"Remember the book THE SECRI [...]
AT ONE WITH THE DIVINE is the RE[...]
these pages, you'll learn exactly how to use the
miraculous power of your Divine connection to heal
anything and everything. This is the information
we've all been waiting for. For lifetimes."
~ **Christiane Northrup, M.D.**
Author: WOMEN'S BODIES, WOMEN'S WISDOM


"Once again Bob Fritchie has chosen to speak the
truth and invite you to awaken to God's love. The
distinction he makes in comparing personal love to
Divine love is monumental. I pray that all who read
this book will be opened to clearly understanding that
we were created to be at one with God, but we must
make a choice to be fully integrated with the Creator
of all. We have been given free will to make the
choice – to open our eyes and hearts and merge fully
with the Creator.
"This book contains information about how to
engage in your own healing through your spiritual self
and picks up where psychology has left off. As a
Christian, I realize that there are ideas herein that
may cause some people to question. Take Bob's
advice and ask the Creator for your own answers and
learn to listen from a stance of love and protection as
you allow Divine love to teach and guide you. Many
blessings await you."
~ **Marsha P. Burdette, Ph.D.**
Licensed Psychologist


"I've attended Bob's Divine Love Healing webinars
for several years now. And I've read all his books.
This last book, Being at One with the Divine, is Bob's
most comprehensive and insightful book. I was so
fascinated by it, I read the whole book in just two
days. I've used Bob's Divine Love Healing on my

clients, my family and friends, and myself. Quite simply, it works!

"I've explored many healing methods over the years, but this is *the most powerful*. And it's also the simplest and easiest to use. I highly recommend this book to anyone seriously interested in healing others or themselves."

**~ John Cali**
Author: *http://www.GreatWesternPublishing.org/*


"Robert Fritchie is a teacher, writer, and healing assistant to the Divine who has blessed him with many gifts. Perhaps the greatest gift that he possesses is his ability to comprehend and explain both spiritual and natural phenomenon with the objectivity that comes with a scientific viewpoint that is immersed in a deep faith. The matters, which he studies and conveys to us in his books, include an understanding of the healing methods that have been practiced by seers, holy men, shamans, and other enlightened ones for many millennia. Nevertheless, scientific thought often runs at odds with spiritual beliefs in today's world. However, Robert has found the path that allows him and us to reconcile these different views of life and the universe, which often appear disparate to many of us.

"Throughout his life, Robert has studied communication systems and healing systems known to our ancient ancestors. As we progress from our remembered past into the future, he takes us along on a journey during which he explains the important matters of life, which we should know and understand as we unite our physical selves with the Divine. Most importantly, he concisely relates and clearly explains this body of knowledge in a way that all of us may comprehend."

**~ John Sase, Ph.D.**
Author: CURIOUS ALIGNMENTS

# Being at One with the Divine

## the Divine

### Self-Healing with Divine Love

by

Robert G. Fritchie

World Service Institute
Knoxville, Tennessee

Disclaimer: The author of this book does not dispense medical advice or prescribe the use of any technique as a form of treatment for physical, emotional, spiritual or medical problems without the advice of a physician, either directly or indirectly. The intent of the author is only to offer information of a nature to help you in your quest for spiritual, emotional and physical well-being. In the event you use the information in this book for yourself, which is your constitutional right, the author, publisher, printer and distributors assume no responsibility for your actions.

Library of Congress Control Number 2013955444

ISBN 978-0-9819513-6-2

Fritchie, Robert G.
Being at One with the Divine
Self Healing with Divine Love
1st edition January 2014

1. Mind and body.    2. Spirituality.    3. Spiritual Healing.
4. Self-Healing Techniques.    5. Self-Help Techniques.

Front Cover design by Robert R. Tatters

Back Cover art and original poetry, "Flower of the Healing Heart"
(c) 2013 by Nicholas Kirsten-Honshin. All rights reserved.
Visit Honshin in his gallery at Tlaquepaque, Sedona, AZ, and on the web at *HonshinFineArt.com*

**May you see the world as it is,
yet interpret it
with the greatest love
and intelligence possible.**

~ Maxine Rede Tatters

# Table of Contents

**Divine Love Healing and Health Practitioners  (Continued)**

**Chapter 6**
**Transitions..119**

**Chapter 7**
**Healing Yourself from Within..135**

## Into the Future (Continued)

## Epilogue..202

## Appendix..207

# Prologue

My intention in writing this book is to provide a comprehensive description of advanced healing techniques that will help you to heal yourself. Physical healing of individuals is but one component of a much broader spectrum. This includes the correction of limited beliefs and false teachings as well as adjustments to mass consciousness, for a better understanding of our environment, our spiritual heritage, and each other.

World Service Institute has already published four healing books that give the reader a blueprint for healing the above topics. Yet, as people rush to implement solutions, they sometimes fail to grasp the fundamentals.

Consequently, when people see evidence of mental or physical changes taking place in people as a result of our healing programs, the casual observer thinks that he is witnessing a miracle.

# BEING AT ONE WITH THE DIVINE

After a student has experienced a healing or has participated in helping others, the student has a better understanding of his or her spiritual birthright.

*Our spiritual birthright is to be able to experience and apply the energy of Divine Love throughout every aspect of our lives.*

There is also a significant change of attitude when a student owns  the healing process and understands that what happened during a healing is not a *miracle*, but rather the relearning of a natural healing method afforded to us by God, the Creator of the universe.

Over the last 33 years, I have helped with a variety of healings on people, places, and things.  Thousands of people have contacted me for healing help because they had serious system disorders or they  were "at the end of their ropes" when conventional medicine was unable to provide solutions.

This book is the story of how some of those people were helped and how you can use our healing systems to increase your knowledge, help you to heal more rapidly, and make your life more enjoyable.

# Chapter 1

# The Scientific Reality
## of
# Divine Love Healing

**Impart as much as you can of
your spiritual being to those
who are on the road with you,
and accept as something
precious what comes back to
you from them.**

~ Albert Schweitzer

# The Scientific Reality of Divine Love Healing

My spiritual journey began with a vision that appeared to me while I was reading a newspaper. First I saw a rotating pyramid, in color, three feet in front of me. Then I heard a voice: "Study energy!"

I was flabbergasted and did not know what to make of the experience; nothing like that had ever happened to me before. My wife said something like, "Let it be whatever it is meant to be!"

Within a short time, I met and became close friends with Dr. Marcel Vogel, senior materials scientist with IBM. Dr. Marcel Vogel and I shared a common goal. That goal was to find ways to help humanity in whichever direction we were led to serve.

In 1979 the only thing in my knowledge base about energy was what was taught in engineering colleges. Engineering students had no concept of and no exposure to "subtle energies."

Vogel became my mentor and introduced me to shamans, energy healers, medicine men, psychics, and energy scientists. Marcel also told me of his own angelic experiences and

# BEING AT ONE WITH THE DIVINE

said that he prayed I would have angelic guidance as we moved forward.

As I went through the early months, quite frankly I wasn't sure what was real and what was not!

I realized that the path I was on was not a normal one. The two things that I had going for me were *dedication* and lack of *fear*. Why that was so, I do not know.

We started working together on the development of therapeutic crystal transducers that could interact with the human energy field. Vogel had invented specially cut quartz crystals that would greatly amplify the energy of a facilitator's body while he was providing a healing service to another person.

> *The increased facilitator energy was very important and necessary. We learned that the healing energy applied* **TO** *a client had to be higher than the energy* **OF** *the client in order for the client's discordant energy to be released. Remember this fact. It will come up many times throughout this book and give you insight into your own healing.*

# The Scientific Reality of Divine Love Healing

My training proceeded in a very organized fashion as progressively more complex cases were presented to me in groups of three. It was obvious that triplicate cases were given so that healing techniques could be perfected and confidence gained in the true reality of what was happening.

We tested several crystal designs in the first three years. Each design had a therapeutic purpose to facilitate better results on complex cases. Using our intuition, we taught ourselves how to use these devices by interacting with human energy fields and extracting whatever was interfering energetically with a person.

We were able to validate that:

*Energy follows thought.*

*Thought can be directed to a target.*

*Healing requires a clear statement of intention.*

*Healing energy can be transmitted at any distance in zero time. Therefore distance is irrelevant.*

Today many of these proofs are taken for granted, but when they were first introduced between 1980 and 1985, many scientists and medical professionals thought the healings were suspect. However, the results spoke for themselves and were confirmed by laboratory testing.

## Scientific Proofs

Let's examine one finding more closely:

***Our work proved that energy can be transmitted through space to a specific target without a time delay.*** *This means that current scientific beliefs are seriously flawed about how energy transfer really works!*

And lest you think that Vogel and his team were crackpots, consider this: *Michelson-Morley proposed in 1887 that there was an energy field in the universe that permeated everything and was everywhere.*

Sadly, since their instrumentation was not sophisticated enough to offer convincing proof, science rejected their theory and continued to proceed along a different path of beliefs.

# The Scientific Reality of Divine Love Healing

Mainstream science believed that space was empty with nothing in it and has continued to foster this incorrect opinion to the world.

The U.S. Air Force repeated the Michelson-Morley experiment and proved that space IS filled with an unnamed energy field. This experiment was described in the August 1986 publication of NATURE, Volume 322.

It seems that Michelson-Morley were correct.

*Wouldn't you think that information this important would have made headlines throughout the world? However, not much was said over this because scientists had for years supported the opposite belief; if these scientists had to admit to the truth, reputations would be destroyed!*

Let's leave this section on a positive note: *We are not limited by any disinformation that has been propagated on mankind.*

We know what to call the *unnamed* energy field. It is *Divine Love* and we will explain throughout this book the various ways that you can interact with this life-giving energy field. For now, know that Divine Love interacts with a spiritual intention, instantly, at any distance.

# BEING AT ONE WITH THE DIVINE

## My Background

People frequently ask about my background. In my professional life as a trained scientist, chemical engineer, senior manager and businessman, my accomplishments in industry and aerospace are known.

What is important to this discussion is that I am a mentally disciplined person firmly anchored in state-of-the-art science and spiritual energy healing.

I have maintained a skepticism in everything I learned from the energy teachers that Vogel sent me to visit and work with. To keep my perspective intact, I decided to proceed with my "new energy studies" with three objectives. Whatever I learned had to be:

1. Repeatable and something that I could actually do myself.

2. Information that I could teach to others. There was no room for speculative "woo-woo" or "believe-me-because-I-said-so."

3. Harmless to myself and the clients.

## The Scientific Reality of Divine Love Healing

# The Energy Research Experiments

In 1980, Dr. Marcel Vogel and six others started a research project to understand and apply the use of therapeutic crystals designed by Marcel to remove energy disturbances in people. I was one of these six original people applying, teaching, and evaluating the therapeutic use of Vogel Healing Crystals.

In the span of six years, our small group made a dramatic impact on the reality of energy medicine. We were able to help facilitate the release of many different illnesses and diseases. In addition, we served the public by conducting week-long and weekend workshops that were taught by Dr. Vogel and me, as well as numerous guest lecturers.

We tried unsuccessfully to introduce these concepts to the medical profession. In fact, Dr. Vogel provided a one-year training program on the use of his healing crystals to 12 M.D.'s in California. I was a regular participant in that training program and offered my research findings as we went through the program.

# BEING AT ONE WITH THE DIVINE

The doctors, while interested, did not firmly apply what they had learned from Dr. Vogel and the original six evaluators. The doctors were concerned that they would be shunned by their constituents. This resulted in very limited use by the 12 doctors of this scientific approach to energy medicine.

In parallel with the M.D. training program, I developed a varied network of healthcare practitioners: M.D.'s, D.O.'s, chiropractors, psychiatrists, psychologists, family counselors, and others intent on making a difference in the world. These people were located in the United States and Canada as my international outreach had not yet begun.

## The Energy Research Laboratory

In 1984, with other volunteers, I helped build a laboratory in San Jose, California. The intent was to provide Dr. Vogel a private lab from which he could direct energy healing research.

The research included advanced applications and designs for Vogel Healing Crystals together with many other energy studies on water and food crops. The lab was filled with very sophisticated equipment obtained from IBM, Stanford University and other sources.

The Scientific Reality of Divine Love Healing

# As You Do Unto Others

This section title is a Bible phrase that Vogel said quite often to visitors. Prior to and during the laboratory years, we noticed that a very interesting thing happened to people who used Vogel crystals in service to others.

*As a facilitator (user of the healing crystal) helped people in need, the facilitator also experienced energy healing in his own body.*

The long-term effect of this was that every facilitator's energy level (frequency) increased, stepwise, over time. We were able to measure these effects in Dr. Vogel's laboratory.

*Let me assure you that the fundamental teachings you read about in this book were rigorously tested and proven in the laboratory and/or during field research.*

# A Lesson In Love

In all of our healing work, we used a loving intention. My early success rate with crystal healing was approximately 80%. However, for

# BEING AT ONE WITH THE DIVINE

reasons I did not understand at the time, some people did not experience a lasting healing.

A turning point both in my life and in the healing work came when my friend Dr. John J. Adams suggested that I change my technique from using my **personal** love to using **Divine Love.** That change in my intention facilitated two incredible differences: faster results and some instantaneous healings!

The success rate went up to about 99%. What I learned from this experience was that:

*A healing facilitator has to be free from any limited beliefs concerning love.*

Dr. Vogel was always working with Divine Love without saying so; I, however, had been working with personal love, mistakenly thinking that I was emulating Dr. Vogel's approach.

*I knew from the above experience that Divine Love had to be integrated into all future healing work if we wanted to achieve maximum results.*

The Scientific Reality of Divine Love Healing

# My Personal Transformation

By 1983 my own body had gone through a healing transformation. I was able to do non-contact healing work without using a crystal device. In effect, my energy limitations had cleared. My body frequency had increased such that my energy level exceeded what I had been able to achieve using the Vogel Healing Crystal.

# Intuition Was Not Enough

Our early crystal healing work was based upon intuition; however, intuition alone was insufficient for what we were doing. In the next chapter we are going to discuss the *spiritual gifts* that were given to me over time and why these gifts are important.

This is the first time that I have discussed spiritual gifts with anyone. There is also the possibility that some of you may misconstrue and misunderstand my intentions, so let me be clear:

*I want each of you who read this book to understand precisely how you can achieve the skills to do exactly the same type of*

# BEING AT ONE WITH THE DIVINE

*spiritual healing work with Divine Love that I have been doing these past years, should you choose to do so. (Crystals are not involved.)*

You need to know that there is a caveat in receiving and applying *spiritual gifts*. Many people become enamored with the idea of learning to use a new device, a new process, or new information to enhance their own power, position, or acceptance by society. I offer this commentary to you to help you bypass the glamour normally associated with anything that might cause you to consider that what you do is *extraordinary*.

*Please understand that there is nothing extraordinary about what you're going to learn in the next chapter. Anyone who has a proper intention of serving his fellow man and the earth will, upon proving himself, be given access to the information needed to help himself and others.*

The beauty of Divine Love healing is that no one can manipulate or misuse the energy process that we teach. Therefore, go forward with enthusiasm and be willing to release all fear. Thereafter, you will experience amazing

# The Scientific Reality of Divine Love Healing

healing in your own life and in the lives of others.

Some of you might think that you need to have spiritual gifts in order to proceed with Divine Love healing. If you operate in a *group* to serve your fellow man, only *one* of you may need to have one or more of the spiritual gifts discussed in the next chapter.

However, if you choose to do individual healing work with your clients or become the facilitator of your own healing group, then it might behoove you to study the next chapter and determine what spiritual gifts you require. The ultimate decision as to what gifts you receive is God the Creator's prerogative.

*One thing is certain: You will be required to eliminate ego from your personality before you are able to receive certain of these spiritual gifts.*

**I never considered a difference
of opinion in politics,
in religion,
in philosophy,
as cause for withdrawing
from a friend.**

~ Thomas Jefferson

# Chapter 2

# Spiritual Gifts

# BEING AT ONE WITH THE DIVINE

**Before you agree to do anything that might add even the smallest amount of stress to your life, ask yourself: What is my truest intention?**

**Give yourself time to let a YES resound within you. When it's right, I guarantee that your entire body will feel it.**

~ Oprah Winfrey

Spiritual Gifts

# Fact or Fiction

It sounds incredible if you are learning for the first time that everyone can do exactly the same things in healing work! *But it is true.* So please don't be impressed by what follows; instead just accept that what we are sharing here can be, and is, directly applicable to you!

*YOU can learn to do everything being talked about in this book. All you have to do is be open to the spiritual nature of things and **ASK** the Creator for what you need. Show the Creator that your requests are for the higher good of all, that you have integrity in what you do, and you will generally be given the spiritual gifts that you ask for when needed.*

It took me several years to develop an *awareness* of what was going on in myself and in my students. It was tough going at first because I did not know what was happening to them *energetically*, or why some people got well and others didn't.

Fortunately, I was born with a high level of curiosity and wanted to know how healing energy worked. I asked the Creator to give

31

me whatever spiritual gifts I needed to help people and nature. Those spiritual gifts appeared when needed. However, I had to learn to use each gift in service to humanity and the earth before receiving another spiritual gift.

## Key Spiritual Gifts

If you choose to facilitate healing in others, you may find that you need some of the following spiritual gifts. Your gifts may be given in a different order than shown below, depending upon what you need.

**My first spiritual gift was Sensing and *Discrimination*.**

This gift was given in two parts:

First, I learned how to ***sense*** anything at a distance. This enabled me to "tune in" to a person and differentiate the person I was seeking from a crowd and even at what distance that person was from me. This was an interesting exercise for me as it *proved to me that what I was doing was real and repeatable.*

# Spiritual Gifts

Second, the **discrimination** component appeared. Discrimination is used in society to describe actions that isolate one group from another. We are not talking here about social issues.

*By "discrimination" we mean that we can all learn to identify an irregular energy in something and then send Divine Love to that person, place or thing to effect change. This is the true reality; when combined with Divine Love and a spirit-based petition for action, the result is usually a change in the subject.*

*The most important application of this two-part gift is the ability **to sense any energy disturbance** in a person.* To help me further develop this particular gift, my angel guidance system helped me to meet a variety of physicians. Those physicians introduced me to their patients, many of whom had life-threatening illnesses.

*I mention this because I was able to determine, based on this gift, whether or not the energy responsible for an individual's illness had left the body when I worked with him energetically. You may also want to be able to discriminate when a healing is really complete.*

It was obvious to me at the time that this concentrated and specific training was being given to me so that Divine Love spiritual healing could be implemented and used in the general population.

**My second spiritual gift was energy sensitivity.**

This gift occurred within days of demonstrating control over the first spiritual gift. *Sensitivity* deals with your ability to sense energy disturbances in another person. This gift was given to me because of my research work in understanding spiritual energy.

Through simple experiments, the angels taught me to identify and detect the presence of what is called *subtle energy.* Today, most everyone can be taught to sense the subtle energy of emotions, but when I started healing work, all of this energy information was unknown to me.

# Spiritual Gifts

There are two parts to *sensitivity*:

## A. Volume control

*You can learn to increase or decrease your sensitivity just as you adjust the volume on a radio.*

*ASK the Creator if you need this gift.*

It may be important for you to learn to do this so that you are not overwhelmed by what you vibrationally sense, particularly if you work in nature. This is needed because every living thing emits a vibration that translates in your body as a tone that you can sense. It is much like being subjected to many musical instruments all playing different notes loudly!

## B. Overcoming Suits Of Armor

To survive in a high-pressure corporate culture that did not tolerate error required my constituents and me to develop emotional *suits of armor*. This armor is a metaphor for not feeling emotional energy in ourselves or other people. In other words, we learned to make tough business decisions under pressure, *without emotion*.

# BEING AT ONE WITH THE DIVINE

Thus, while we were able to make complex and difficult decisions with relative ease, it was evident to me that I had lost contact with the feelings of other people. This insulation factor was still present when I first started to awaken spiritually.

It took several months to dissolve my protective armor and realize that I was actually measuring a very subtle energy. In the beginning I could not sense energy in a person.

Medical professionals are also known to armor their emotions to enable themselves to function in chaotic situations. Most doctors are unable to feel energy until they learn how to trust their spiritual selves. Another factor is that most M.D.'s do not have any training in sensing subtle energy in their patients, so they question the reality of what happens in energy healing.

In the late 1970's, other pioneering health care professionals came forth and taught sensing and the application of healing energy. Their activities helped legitimatize the art of energy healing.

# Spiritual Gifts

Students in my workshops had to learn quickly how to *sense* and *measure* energy to validate their own abilities.  Otherwise, the energy teachings being presented by us could not be confirmed.

*The spiritual gift of sensing enabled me to help my students engage in educational experiments.*

*Once you accept that you can sense objects and people, then you are ready to learn how to do various kinds of healing work.*

You might be inclined to question whether or not *sensing* and *sensitivity* are *spiritual gifts* or simply *learned skills*.  Let's find out by sensing water energy.

## An Intention Experiment

You will need to hold your breath for awhile, so please read all the instructions below before starting the experiment.

1. Get two *empty*, same-sized, water glasses.

2. *Take a deep breath and hold it*.  Fill both glasses full of water.

# BEING AT ONE WITH THE DIVINE

3. Place one glass on the kitchen counter.

4. Place the other glass on a table at least 20 feet from the first glass.

5. Go back to the first glass and *let out your breath gently*.

6. Breathe softly for a minute to recover your breathing.

7. Look at the first glass of water, *draw in and hold your breath*. Hold the thought of sending the water your *personal love energy* and **pulse** your breath to send the thought into the water. (*Pulsing* is letting your breath out sharply through your nose as if you were clearing your nostrils.)

8. *Take another deep breath and hold it*. Using your open hand, *tell yourself to sense the energy coming from the side of the glass.*

9. Measure how far your *personal love* radiates sideways from the outside surface of the glass.

10. *Then breathe out slowly*.

11. Write down your answer.

# Spiritual Gifts

You will learn that your *personal love* energy field may extend from several inches to several feet from the glass. With a little practice, you can learn to *sense* very accurately how far in space the energy field projects from the glass.

When you breathe in and hold breath, your energy field is pulled in near the surface of your skin. And when you breathe out, your body energy expands outward from your skin.

The purpose of holding breath while measuring is to *pull in* your energy field so that it does not mingle with the energy field radiating from the water. If you happen to breathe while in proximity to the water, the charge in the water glass may transfer to you, making your measurement inaccurate.

For the second glass of water:

1. Draw in and hold your breath. Leave the first glass and *go to the second glass*.

2. Hold the thought of sending *Divine Love energy* into the water and **pulse** your breath to send the thought into the water.

3. Back away from the second glass about 10 feet and breathe a few times.

# BEING AT ONE WITH THE DIVINE

4. Then *draw in and hold breath again*. Slowly approach the glass, then with your open hand, sense how far the energy field of *Divine Love* radiates from the side of the second glass towards you.

5. Then breathe normally and record results.

Did you notice that the energy of *Divine Love* radiated much further from the glass compared to *personal love*?

Once you have mastered sensing water energy, the next step is to apply what you have learned to human beings. S*ensing* is very useful in identifying the presence of an energy field emitted from a person, an animal, or something else on earth, such as the air, plants, or bodies of water.

*Sensing* energy radiating from water in a glass is a learned skill; the activity of sensing *into a person* is a spiritual *sensitivity* gift.

Ask a friend who has a health symptom to help you. Use your *sensitivity* to find the exact location of the root cause of their *symptom*. If you can do this accurately, then you have the gift already. If not, then you will need to ASK for the gift should you need this capability.

# Spiritual Gifts

**My third spiritual gift was *telepathy.***

To expedite my training, it was clear that questions needed to be asked and answers received. In the beginning, I would ask "yes" and "no" questions and receive a pulse in my third eye for a "yes" answer. (The *third eye* is an energy center called a "chakra" that is located between your eyebrows.)

This was too time-consuming and limiting. I wanted to be able to have a free-verse conversation wherein I could drill down into any subject matter and understand what was happening.

One day, I just asked an open-ended question that could not be answered by a pulsed *yes* or *no*. Suddenly, I heard a voice answering me with specific information based upon my question. When this happened, I was grateful.

I asked the voice to identify itself and tell me what it represented; t*he answer became one of the first steps to my own spiritual awakening.*

The voice said that it was my Guardian Angel assigned to me by God, the Creator of all things. More importantly, the Angel explained

# BEING AT ONE WITH THE DIVINE

to me that my purpose on earth was to teach people how to function with Divine Love in both healing work and in daily living.

I suddenly started to awaken spiritually and was able to recall many of my own past life experiences. Until this awakening happened, there had been no interest on my part in the concept of past lives.

*Past lives* was a new wrinkle in my education, so let's explore this concept a bit more. My early upbringing in a Christian faith taught that man is born and lives one life on earth. When you die, you are rewarded by going to Heaven where you live in a spiritual form and all is peaceful, loving and well. Or you go to a place called Hell where you suffer for eternity.

As the spiritual recall of my own past lives increased, it became apparent to me that we do cycle through many lifetimes. One of my past lives involved Dr. Vogel. When I asked him about it, he confirmed our past association with information that we had previously not discussed - but both knew!

Since that experience many years ago, I continue to confirm past life associations with many people from all walks of life.

## Spiritual Gifts

Today I have no doubt about the reality of past lives.

*Find your own truth.  ASK  the Creator of the universe to reveal your spiritual truth to you.*

## Ego Elimination

A few words about eliminating personal ego is appropriate at this point.  Since 1979 I have been in close communication with six different angels who *specialize* in various topics.  This is not a misprint; angels have areas of expertise just like we humans do!

Lest you think that my angel communications were all enjoyable, let me assure you that they were decidedly not.  *Tough love* was evident in everything they did.  The first five years were filled with confrontational discussions that forced me to deal with myself and to help me to let go of my ego.  One day I asked the angels why they were pushing me so hard in the manner in which we interacted.

*I was told that it was important for me to learn how to function without attachment to results, fame, or fortune.*

43

# BEING AT ONE WITH THE DIVINE

I really took this advice to heart. I had seen how some companies became greedy in order to generate huge profits and how it often compromised the integrity of managers whose decisions were driven by financial rewards.

## My fourth spiritual gift was *knowing*.

Throughout history there are many people, generally ordinary folks, who have had this gift. *Knowing* means that you can learn about anything you seek by accessing information through your own spiritual essence.

*Knowing* comes from within you. You also know that the information is 100% accurate because you test for the truth from within yourself.

Let me explain this further, as it is important that you deal with truth that is *spiritually* and *physically* true. Some topics can be true *spiritually*, but not true in your *physical* life!

*Don't believe everything you are told.*

*Always verify under what conditions the information that you receive is true.*

# Spiritual Gifts

My angels gave me a difficult time learning about *knowing*. They did this by making partially true statements and waiting to see if I could detect any discrepancies. As my accuracy improved, the statements became more complex.

*Once I learned to surrender control of my mind to the guidance of my spirit, my accuracy became 100% in determining the spiritual and physical truth of anything. I strongly suggest that you learn to surrender your entire being to the guidance of God, the Creator of the universe.*

Another angelic objective was for me to become dependent upon my own spirit rather than needing angelic support. This is an important statement because many people have difficulty trusting their own spirit and prefer to be enamored by the idea that an angel will do their thinking for them.

*Angels will give you information and give you alternatives, but no angel wants to control your thinking.*

# BEING AT ONE WITH THE DIVINE

It is very difficult for most people to surrender their intellect to their *spiritual self*.   Your *spiritual self (your personal internal spirit)* has an awareness level much higher than intuition alone.   What we think is often *mental intuition* that can be compromised by intellect; *spiritual intuition* appears from within us as a *knowing* that is accurate and cannot be compromised. Accepting this idea was a personal struggle of mine for several years.

*However, once I learned that my spirit would never deceive me, it opened new opportunities for information retrieval.*

I was eventually able to *tune in* and go back to any event, *now* or in the *past,* to learn the truth about something I was interested in.   In fact, some of the information that I give to you throughout this book is a result of my direct personal knowledge of spiritual truth.

I do not expect you to believe everything that is written here.   Be a skeptic, but stay open to spiritual understanding.

*I encourage you to validate whatever you can to establish your own spiritual truths.*

### Spiritual Gifts

*Remember this:*

*There are things occurring in the universe that are spiritually true, whether or not you or I believe them!*

If you choose to claim your spiritual birthright and ask for the gift of *knowing*, you will learn to *know* a spiritual truth when one is presented to you. Then you will be able to ascertain what to believe in.

## The Past, the Present and the Future

One of the most important things that I would like to share with you is this: The **past** *is like a documented history book.* Unfortunately, the accuracy of documented historical events is often altered in accordance with the beliefs of the writers.

However, when you operate as a *spiritual human being* and apply your spiritual gifts, you can access historic information accurately and use it to help mankind and the earth. As a spiritually wise person, you will also avoid making poor decisions in the *present*.

# BEING AT ONE WITH THE DIVINE

*The **present** is defined as today, right now, this moment.*

*When you access information relative to the present, be aware that scenarios and outcomes can be changed based upon whatever actions people take **in** the present, e.g., physical truths can change.*

Another realization about the **present** (and the **future***)* is that events can be changed by a *small group of people* utilizing their own spirit and Divine Love.

*Acting in conjunction with a spiritual petition, you and your group can activate petitions that can change the present and the future.*

*In other words, we do not need to be held captive by a forecast event; we do not need to be afraid of the future.*

The **future** *represents a kaleidoscope of possibilities.* You can listen to many self-proclaimed prophets offering viewpoints on what is to happen. For example, you may recall a number of authors and lecturers who announced that the earth would either end or be visibly changed in December 2012. Yet no significant *physical* changes occurred relative to most stated prophesies.

The only change that I noticed is that the energy of Divine Love increased significantly in 2012. Divine Love is currently stabilized at a much higher vibration level than it was even two years ago.

We will explain how you can contribute to making *needed changes* in Chapter 4 (Mass Consciousness). But first, in the next chapter, we'll examine some foundational concepts that should help you to better understand Divine Love healing.

# BEING AT ONE WITH THE DIVINE

**Ask and it will be given to you;
seek and you will find;
knock and the door
will be opened to you.**

~ Jesus Christ

# Chapter 3

# Evolution of Divine Love Healing

**If someone tells you
who they are, believe them.**

~ Maya Angelou

# Evolution of Divine Love Healing

This chapter is about how the Divine Love Group Healing Process (DLGHP) became the core teaching found in our well-received self-healing webinar, *Healing Yourself From Within*. This webinar also draws upon the many principles taught in our three healing books: SURVIVING CHAOS, APPLY YOUR BIRTHRIGHT, and ACCELERATE YOUR SPIRITUAL HEALING.

There are significant differences between the original DLGHP coursework that taught a group how to facilitate a healing in a client and today's *Healing Yourself From Within Webinars* that teach clients how to heal themselves *without group participation*. The latter has become possible because of the huge frequency shift in Divine Love that we will examine later.

## Transition to the DLGHP

The transition point that caused me to shift emphasis and start teaching group healing work was motivated by an experience given to me by a small child. A mother had brought her child to a doctor's office where I was doing healing work. The child had been vomiting for two days and was still in a dry heaving state. I had been asked to help the child, but the

# BEING AT ONE WITH THE DIVINE

mother wanted her son helped without using a healing crystal because of her religious beliefs. I put my healing crystal aside in compliance with her wishes.

I sensed that the child thought that his parents did not love him. As soon as I picked up the child, I felt a rush of energy going into him. I told him that his mother and father loved him. That was all it took; his stomach retching stopped. He jumped off my lap and skipped out of the room with a big smile on his face!

The *spontaneous healing* the child experienced certainly surprised me. I realized that it was time to start teaching people to do healing work without crystals.

When I told Dr. Vogel what happened, he encouraged me to continue teaching with and without a crystal. He said:

*"All people who provide service will clear their bodies and become human crystals."*

Over the years, I found his statement to be totally true.

I was becoming concerned that the applicable scientific healing techniques that evolved from crystal healing work were not reaching enough people. I also noticed that most people were mainly interested in healing without crystals. That is why in 1985 I developed and began teaching the DLGHP. My objective was to share all that we had learned with people in a manner that did not require devices of any kind.

# Simple Beginnings

The healing techniques known to be true were compiled into the DLGHP for the general public. This Process was taught through workshops in the United States and Canada. Our program was quite simple:

A group of volunteers were assembled in *one location* to help a client in need.

We placed the client on a chair in the middle of a circle of seated volunteers.

The volunteers held an intention of sending Divine Love to the client in the circle while that client recited a Divine Love healing petition that contained his or her intention for healing.

## BEING AT ONE WITH THE DIVINE

Volunteers continued to send Divine Love to the client until the lead person for the group determined (through sensing) that the client healing was complete.

Nothing earth shaking there, right? Wrong!

There were problems as small groups tried to implement the Process on their own AFTER they had been through a workshop. The problem stumped me for several months; then I had an epiphany!

*The problems people were having in their own small groups did not happen during a large group workshop. In a workshop, we continued to send Divine Love to a client in the room with us until that client's energy field was cleared of the condition being addressed.*

*It did not matter what the client's illness was; almost all of the clients responded to healing.*

*A major finding was that the smaller groups often did not wait long enough for the healing to complete in a client before a group disengaged.*

## Evolution of Divine Love Healing

In discussing problem healings with the actual clients, we learned that a few clients struggled with issues concerning the Creator, their personal belief structures, and their ability to take in and experience Divine Love. Some of these conflicted issues also slowed their healing.

How could I modify the initial Process so that people did not have to struggle? Reflecting over the prior five years of intense crystal healing experiences, it was evident that there were many *subtle techniques* that could be extracted and applied directly in the DLGHP.

To help you understand what components we planned to extract, following is a quick overview on how I taught crystal healing.

## Vogel Healing Crystal Overview

The major steps were:

A facilitator would ask a client if he wanted to release a proclaimed **symptom**. If the answer was "No," we stopped right there and did not go further.

# BEING AT ONE WITH THE DIVINE

If the answer was "Yes," the facilitator would connect the crystal to the energy field of the client at the client's **thymus** using a non-contact proprietary technique.

Then the facilitator would ask the client to draw in and **hold breath** while the client **focused** on the **root cause** of the illness.

We asked the client to **spiritually observe** the **root cause** of the **symptom**. This was done not as an exercise in guesswork, but rather as a spiritual acknowledgment of the cause. Sometimes a client would know the **root cause** and other times there would not be any conscious recognition.

Next, the facilitator would issue a sharp **audible command** to the client to "**Release**" (the root cause with a strong pulsed breath) while the facilitator simultaneously snapped the hand holding the crystal away from the client. **This action extracted the energetic root cause of a symptom**.

*When discordant energy is removed, the effect on the human body is similar to physical surgery. There is an energetic wound that needs to be closed, just as a surgeon would close a physical operation.*

## Evolution of Divine Love Healing

The facilitator would help close the energetic wound by holding a healing crystal against the client's chest, directly over the **thymus**. The facilitator would place his empty hand on the client's shoulder or back. The client would be asked to breathe deeply several times, bringing in **Divine Love**, until the client's energy field had come together.

**Note the bold words above. They are some of the components incorporated into the DLGHP.**

## DLGHP Components

Specific components from crystal healing that were added initially to the DLGHP are discussed below. We will include the important components that contributed to both the original Divine Love Group Healing Process and to our current *Healing Yourself From Within Webinar* self-healing process.

In a later chapter, we will examine the importance of specific wording found in the Petitions. We found that if you state your spiritual intention clearly and precisely, you are more apt to receive what you seek.

# BEING AT ONE WITH THE DIVINE

## 1. Symptom vs. Diagnosis

This is one of the most important discoveries we made in developing Petitions. *Some words matter!*

Consider that we serve an audience of people in more than 50 countries, many of whom do not have English as their first language. Most people understand the basic concepts of spiritual energy healing because we strive to make the language clear.

A Divine Love Petition is a precise statement of what you want to have happen. A Petition usually contains a *symptom*.

Symptoms are generally considered to be synonymous with a medical diagnosis. *A "symptom" as we use it is NOT a medical diagnosis unless it is absolutely verified by a reliable lab test that does not have false positives. A symptom, to us, is an indication of how you feel, such as:*

"My head hurts," NOT "My concussion," "My migraine headache," etc.

"I have a runny nose" or "My sinus is stuffed," NOT "I have environmental allergies."

## Evolution of Divine Love Healing

"I am very angry," NOT "I have an anger disorder."

Use "joint pain," NOT "arthritis" or "tendinitis" as your symptom.

Use "ringing in my ears" NOT "tinnitus."

*Another reason that you should not use a diagnosis is that while the medical diagnosis may be completely supported by a valid medical test, THE DIAGNOSIS MAY NOT BE THE ROOT CAUSE OF YOUR PROBLEM.*

Here is a report from a woman who had suffered from back pain:

*"It is always so great and amazing to attend your webinars. I always learn something new and I feel that Divine Love is always around me. Thank you.*

*"I was told by the doctors that I have a gene called HLA B27. This gene attacks my own body, causing, among other symptoms, back pain (I was suffering only back pain).*

# BEING AT ONE WITH THE DIVINE

*"I started the petitions by sending Divine Love to the gene itself and I did not get great results.*

*"So I changed to an Unlovingness Petition with the symptom:* **Back Pain.** *I repeated the petition around 6 times during the day for a couple of days.*

*"By the time I attended the webinar, the pain had subsided a lot and now it is completely gone. Thank you so much for your invaluable help!"*
*~ R.O., Buenos Aires, Argentina*

Note that R.O. started with the medical diagnosis, but only got results when she used the *actual physical symptom* in her Petition!

Remember:
*If you use the wrong symptom, nothing may happen!*

Many times people with multiple symptoms fall into this trap thinking that a common medical term used to describe a symptom is preferred to using the physical symptom itself.

*Therefore always use what you experience in your own body in non-medical terms.*

## 2. The Role of the Thymus

Previously we did not make an issue about where a problem was located in a body because we utilized the client's *thymus*. Vogel had determined that the thymus gland distributed energy throughout the body. *Thus, all healing work could be accomplished by simply having a client focus upon his own thymus.*

For example, if you had something wrong with your big toe, you might be inclined to work directly on that toe using whatever healing modality you chose. In our work, we use the client's thymus and let the client's thymus redirect energy to the toe. This saves a lot of unnecessary effort on the part of both the facilitator and the client.

*We ask clients to focus on the thymus in the DLGHP.*

## 3. Root Causes

*This is a major component that cannot be overemphasized.*

# BEING AT ONE WITH THE DIVINE

*Modern medical practice does not eliminate the energetic root cause of a symptom; medicine treats the effect. For example, pain medicine can suppress a headache, but that medicine seldom releases the root cause of the headache. So while we can numb ourselves to not feel any pain, we miss a big opportunity because our body is trying to tell us that something is wrong that requires our attention.*

*By having a client address the **root cause of a symptom** in a DLGHP petition, **the root cause can be released**.*

In the early development of the *DLGHP*, I experimented with leaving out any reference to *root causes*. Sometimes, healing would occur; on other occasions, a strange phenomenon developed:

*A client would release one problem only to substitute a brand new problem!*

For example, if a client came to a group with a drug addiction and was released from that addiction, the client would sometimes adopt another bad habit, such as binge eating. Or a client might manifest an entirely *new* behavior, such as smoking, when previously smoking had not been an issue.

It did not take me long to realize that:

*The substitute condition occurred because the client had not released **all the root causes** of the initial symptom.*

*This single fact is why we constructed very broad petitions, so that we could include **all possible root causes** in our petitions.*

*When we did this properly, client healings progressed rapidly to desired solutions. And the healings were permanent!*

## 4. Audible Release of Petitions

While the reason is not totally understood, the **spoken** word has power that can make a substantial difference in results. This is why we ask clients to state petitions **aloud**.

*I believe that a verbal statement not only informs every cell in the body what is happening, but also transmits a signal to the energy of mind, so that the mind doesn't prevent the healing.*

# BEING AT ONE WITH THE DIVINE

## 5. Breath Pulse

A breath pulse at the end of stating a Petition **aloud** was always incorporated in the DLGHP. In my experience, if a breath pulse is not done, healing continues more slowly.

*Understand that you are composed of many energy fields that do not stop at your skin surface.* You actually radiate in space from several inches to several feet from your body! Therefore, the act of healing includes both the *internal* and *external* you.

The act of pulsing your breath performs two functions:

*1. It releases the petition (which is a directed intention) into space so that the petition acts on the body from the outside in.* Without the breath pulse, a Petition acts to heal a client internally first, and then moves outward from the core of the body. The true value is that most energy that impacts us starts from the outside, so it makes sense to start healing from the outside.

*2. The second effect of a pulsed breath is to inform the entire cell structure in a person's body that a Divine Love petition has activated.*

## Evolution of Divine Love Healing

Dr. Vogel told me once that he believed the act of pulsing breath first compressed, and then released, compression on the spinal column which in turn transmitted the held thought (the Petition) to every cell in the body.

### 6. Closing the Energetic Field

In group work, a client receives Divine Love from the group until the energetic problem is resolved. Divine Love fills the client's "surgical hole" and heals the entire area automatically.

*The same thing happens when you use the **Healing Yourself From Within self-healing** techniques when you are working by yourself.*

## Confusion Factors

Divine Love healing is simple to implement if we use the correct keys to unlock the mysteries of healing. As people learn how energy healing works, they are astounded because it is so simple.

*There are no special gadgets, no special facility, and no rigorous beliefs required.*

# BEING AT ONE WITH THE DIVINE

However, you need to grasp the fundamentals if you want to know how to be successful in healing work. To begin, we will try to explain the differences between *personal love, Divine Love* and *mind healing.*

## Divine Love vs. Personal Love

***Using personal love in healing work is the most critical mistake that you can make!***

The above statement may come as a surprise. People are taught many variations for a definition of love, but believe me when I tell you that using personal love is the spiritual, mental, and physical downfall of people doing healing work.

> *If any facilitator becomes emotionally embroiled in a client's energy problems, he unknowingly stores the client's energy in himself.*

If the facilitator does not clear his own system following a client healing, the facilitator's energy field continues to store the emotions and energetic experiences of ALL his clients. Over time, the health of the facilitator begins to deteriorate as the facilitator's system shuts down.

# Evolution of Divine Love Healing

*In my experience, there is a "point of no return," whereby a facilitator in such a health crisis can only be helped by the direct intervention of the Creator.*

Worse still is the situation where *a* facilitator tries to **force** healing using his personal love; this is especially common between parents and children. That is why our Petitions include a clause asking "for healing according to the Creator's will." This important clause prevents a facilitator from trying to force a solution based upon **desire**, rather than by functioning in cooperation with the Divine.

*In my experience, when a healing does not occur, it is because there may be one or more spiritual conditions that need to be released before a symptom releases.*

There are three major differences between personal love and Divine Love. Definitions and limitations are covered in my other books and summarized below:

## Unconditional Love

Divine Love is unconditional; there is nothing special that you must do to operate with Divine

## BEING AT ONE WITH THE DIVINE

Love.   Some educators today suggest that mankind is not able to operate unconditionally because our personalities are hard-wired to apply conditions to everything we do.  I agree with this if one is operating with *the power of mind*.

However, in using the DLGHP we are operating with **internal spirit,** not the mind.  When we use a Petition referencing **spirit***,* we eliminate any mental intention and instead automatically operate with **spiritual** intention.  Then we can do healing unconditionally.

### Judgmental Love

*Divine Love is NOT judgmental.*   The Creator does not judge, but you may be inadvertently judging yourself or others.   Operating with judgmental love can create problems because you form an energetic link between yourself and the client.

*That link can be so powerful that your energy level may plummet as the client draws on your energy to become well.*

# Evolution of Divine Love Healing

## Emotional Love

Divine Love is a *spiritual neutral energy,* free from any emotion. Personal love is emotional on many levels and it can create an environment for various energy problems to manifest within you.

## An Assessment

One of my students, S.Y. from Canada, wrote to me in September 2013:

"The concept of Divine Love being neutral was definitely presented in the meeting, which I definitely heard, [and] had the idea  it was understood; but it wasn't until last week that it really sunk in.  *Then it became somewhat troubling to accept.*

"It's the word LOVE, which in my usage, could only be good, positive, an actively flowing and warm verb-like essence. *The idea of it being neutral seemed inert, stagnant, beige, a lifeless blob*. It took a few pondering days, but now I might be getting closer, imagining current, breath, pulse, waves and other nouns that place neutrality as a what-is totality within a picture I recognize.

71

# BEING AT ONE WITH THE DIVINE

"All habitual thinking can constitute a perceptual block.

"I am not sure it's completely dissolved *[her misunderstanding of Divine Love,]* but it is less solid at least."

This heartfelt note reveals a concept many of us grew up with: that all love is the same or must fit our preconceived idea of what love is.

*To function with Divine Love requires us to open ourselves to a new way of loving called Spiritual Love.*

## Spiritual Love

*By definition, Spiritual Love IS Divine Love. Many people think that "Spiritual Love" and "Divine Love" are concepts. They are not concepts; they are the true reality.*

Some people have been taught to seek the spiritual kingdom of God externally. *Yet every human being is already a spiritual being* who can operate with Divine Love to enjoy life here on earth and become free from suffering and emotional illness. I believe that most suffering is optional and is not a requirement for living.

## Change Your Thinking

As stated earlier, if you are a facilitator, your *emotional, judgmental,* or *conditional* love may cause your client's emotional energy to be stored in yourself. *How long do you think you can operate in this manner before you become very ill?*

If you are personally judgmental right now, or act with conditional love towards others or yourself, it is unlikely that you will achieve any self-healing until you decide to release these behaviors.

*Once you learn to operate with Divine Love in all things that you do in your life, you avoid energy conditions that limit your health and effectiveness in helping yourself and your fellow man.*

## Mind Blocks

*It is my experience that the mind, itself a subtle energy body, does not discriminate between energy changes that are good for you and energy changes that are bad for you.*

73

# BEING AT ONE WITH THE DIVINE

Therefore, if you do not tell your body what is happening, the mind very often blocks the flow of all energy changes in your system. Then the discordant energy trying to leave your system is prevented from exiting by your own mind! This principle has been repeatedly proven in hundreds of cases.

> *In every case where the body is not informed at the cellular level, healings occur slowly and in some cases not at all.*

Recent medical research on thought energy in the brain shows on a computer monitor where different thoughts are stored in the brain, but what about the *mind*?

> *Do you believe all thought is stored in the brain?*

> *I used to believe the mind was contained exclusively in the brain, but it is not. The mind also envelops the body in space around the entire body and is also layered inside the body like an onion.*

I was once asked to help a woman who had been in a serious traffic accident. Her husband told me that she could no longer carry on a normal conversation.

# Evolution of Divine Love Healing

She spoke to me in an animated nervous fashion. Her words were spoken clearly, but her sentence structure was so mixed up that a listener could not determine what the woman was talking about.

I knew that it was likely that the impact of the crash had energetically imprinted her system and caused the malfunction. When my hand passed slowly through the space surrounding her body with the intention of detecting problems in her mind, I could sense random sentence segments.

Once I realized that what was being sensed were scrambled words and phrases, a pattern emerged. It was then possible to rearrange the phrases on paper by putting them into a logical order. Then we could observe what she was thinking!

What emerged was that, at the time of the accident, she had been troubled by an argument with her husband and she was also concerned by another family problem.

*After a healing was conducted to release the thought imprints, she recovered her normal speech and thought processes. Hopefully, researchers will take note of*

# BEING AT ONE WITH THE DIVINE

*this testimony and expand research to include mind energy in and around the body.*

*The mind is a living hologram that stores thoughts, similar to how the hard drive on your computer stores programs.*

To measure stored mental thought we would need to apply measurement technology in a three-dimensional analysis, so that thought patterns from both brain and mind can be seen simultaneously on display devices.

# DLGHP:  Refined Practices

## 1. Soul vs. Spirit

In our early DLGHP workshops, we spent considerable time evaluating the best ways to operate, be it with *Soul* or with *Spirit*.  We found that the concept of using individual *Soul* produced fairly good results.  However, I was bothered by all the confusion in literature concerning the differences between the *Soul* and the *Spirit* of an individual.  Which one led to the best outcome?

# Evolution of Divine Love Healing

We determined through trial and error that when volunteers used their individual internal *Spirit* to facilitate group work, client results were achieved more quickly and sometimes produced a *spontaneous healing*. We also observed that it took fewer people using *Spirit* to facilitate a complex healing.

Note: When 40 or 50 people in a group work with their internal *Spirit*, rather than their *Soul*, that group can perform a massive healing on persons, places, or things, at any distance and over a wide area. The results produced can be amazing. You will see how this becomes important when we discuss healing in the mass consciousness chapter.

Over a three-year period we investigated how many people it took to achieve results in a variety of circumstances  Since the addition of people to a group produces an exponential effect, it was of keen interest to all of us to determine how many people were needed for particular problem solving.

Generally, 10 people were sufficient for DLGHP group healing work;  mass consciousness work required more, depending upon the objective.

# BEING AT ONE WITH THE DIVINE

## 2. Addition Of Distance Healing

Both Marcel and I had done considerable distant healing work with individuals located throughout the United States. We did not teach distant healing in workshops for many years because we wanted people to first grasp the reality of localized healing before adding complexity to their understanding.

It was difficult for people to comprehend and accept that we could all use Divine Love in a group setting to effect a healing. Many students were like me; they had not had exposure to spiritual healing.

Nevertheless, after several years of teaching DLGHP healing work, students began to approach me for healing help for a friend or relative in a distant town. This was good because it meant that people were ready to broaden their reality. Until then, many people had heard a great deal about *distant healing,* but considered it a special skill belonging to a select few.

*When I told students in our workshops that everyone could do distant healing, there was an immediate request to apply the concepts to loved ones and animals wherever they were located.*

# Evolution of Divine Love Healing

Beginning in 2009, I taught some of my students how they could do distant healing by telephone to serve clients anywhere in the world. This was the beginning of World Service Institute's international outreach effort.

## 3. Angel Assistance

The reality of angels has been perceived with various levels of skepticism. Although nearly everyone says they believe in angels, many do not readily believe that they can communicate with their angels.

By 2009 we had moved the DLGHP training to the Internet. We allowed people to download my DLGHP course for several months, as I was busy writing SURVIVING CHAOS. Requests for healing help poured in from all over the world after the publication of SURVIVING CHAOS, and we were soon overwhelmed.

We asked the angels to help us and they agreed, so several of my friends and I put together *a Free Healing Program* which anyone can sign up for and use. That program has all the updated components of the DLGHP. And it is supported 24/7 by a combined group of volunteers, both human beings and angels.

# BEING AT ONE WITH THE DIVINE

In 2010 we introduced the *Energy Healing Training Program Webinar.* A key part of that program included introducing students to their angels.

*Students were always amazed to learn that they could have both a spiritual relationship and telepathic contact with their angels.*

*The course awakened people to the reality of angels and the importance of the unseen world.*

We will discuss angel contributions more in upcoming chapters.

**I want you to know that in addition to your own spirit, YOU have one or more angels that you can depend upon!**

**Make your spirit and angels your best buddies!**

When you learn to work with your spirit and Divine Love, you can achieve your full potential because your spirit will always direct you to your higher truth.

# Benefits Summary: DLGHP Healing

The benefits of group healing extend beyond the obvious in that you can work with a group of volunteers to potentially improve health. Inherent in the teachings are other astounding facts:

The DLGHP is a spiritual, not a mental process.

Everyone can do distant healing!

Everyone can participate in a group. Even seriously sick people with low energy levels can help without adversely affecting their own health.

Group volunteers often report healing within themselves while serving others!

The client can be located anywhere in the world; so can the healing group volunteers!

If personal love is used by the volunteer group, results are limited in the client.

We have determined through extensive field testing that *Divine Love can heal all things in people.*

## BEING AT ONE WITH THE DIVINE

We have also learned that the combined energy of a group works exactly the same way in every case. All the volunteer group has to do is send Divine Love to a subject with a spiritual petition of intention.

If the subject is a client (recipient of a healing), then that client recites aloud one of our healing petitions.

If the subject is a place or animal, then the group spokesperson recites the petition.

When the group energy is high enough, the conditions associated with the subject can be changed as the group recites the intended petition. An example is the purification of contaminated food or drinking water.

## Divine Love Healing: The Real Science

In this chapter we have explained the underlying science behind spiritual energy healing with Divine Love. The ability to work with Divine energies is a spiritual birthright. Individuals can experience their own personal transformation, obtain the spiritual gifts they need, and help create positive change in the world.

## Evolution of Divine Love Healing

People from all over the world simultaneously report spontaneous healing during all of our live webinars, regardless of topic. Headaches, chronic pain, depression, and a wide variety of other symptoms have been healed.

*Divine Love Healing is not subject to the limitations of earthbound physics since people can be healed spontaneously at any distance, or over a period of time, depending upon their health condition.*

## Want Proof of Divine Love Healing?

On the main page of the World Service Institute website you will find *Divine Love Healing Reports* written in the words of people who have experienced profound healing. Their testimonies cover the period 2009 to date.

**The report results are real and you can achieve similar results.**

**Once you accept the reality of the reports, you are then ready to pursue advanced healing knowledge.**

We will start with an explanation of the phenomenon of Mass Consciousness.

# BEING AT ONE WITH THE DIVINE

**Whether one believes
in a religion or not,
and whether one believes
in rebirth or not,
there isn't anyone
who doesn't appreciate
kindness and compassion.**

~ Dalai Lama

# Chapter 4

# Correcting
# Mass Consciousness

**Man learns through experience, and the spiritual path is full of different kinds of experiences.**

**He will encounter many difficulties and obstacles, and they are the very experiences he needs to encourage and complete the cleansing process.**

~ Sai Baba

Correcting Mass Consciousness

# The Mass Consciousness Webinars

In 2009, we established a website for World Service Institute. People wrote to me asking how to correct various world conditions that are destroying the earth. Requests ranged from specific things like chemical pollution to issues about how to increase awareness of various topics. This led to the formation of a small volunteer group to implement changes to what is called *Mass Consciousness*.

We initiated a weekly *Mass Consciousness Webinar* to show people how they could apply the principles described in the two books APPLY YOUR BIRTHRIGHT and SURVIVING CHAOS to influence the mass consciousness.

Word spread fast: Group volunteers from 19 countries attended, with anywhere from 10 to 50 volunteers on each webinar.

# Understanding Mass Consciousness

For many years people have talked about the elusive topic of mass consciousness. Many theories have been advanced as to what it is.

# BEING AT ONE WITH THE DIVINE

Some educators believe that consciousness is *spiritual awareness*. We support that idea.

Others believe that the mass consciousness is a big energy database or energetic repository that collects human thoughts somewhere in space. This is not a wild idea that someone just dreamed up; mass consciousness has existed since man had his first thoughts.

> *We teach people to think of the mass consciousness as a collection of energy thought bubbles, sort of what you would see if you looked at a bubble bath. There would be an individual bubble for every unique topic discussed throughout the world, be it spiritual or mental.*

When you think about it this way, each bubble would be gigantic! And there would be billions upon billions. . . In fact, we need a new term to describe *bubble size* because the mass consciousness has been there forever.

It is almost unfathomable to accept the idea that there are energetic thought bubbles surrounding the earth that may have been there since man had a first thought! We cannot comprehend the volume, complexity

## Correcting Mass Consciousness

and number of these bubbles; the number is simply too huge!

So let's create a new word to represent a gigantic number that we can't otherwise describe.

We will call that number the "quadraquippy."

While individual quadraquippy bubbles exist in space everywhere, they congregate together for a given topic.  Since we are defining the *quadraquippy* as a huge number, it might be more convenient to think of an individual belief system as a single quadraquippy bubble that contains all the associated thoughts about that single belief system.

Thus, when people form a new belief system, it too immediately becomes a new quadraquippy bubble resident in the mass consciousness.  As more people fortify that same belief system, the quadraquippy energy bubble intensifies and grows larger.

### Why the concern?

*Mass consciousness quadraquippy bubbles are "energy packets" that can influence the thinking process of anyone.*

# BEING AT ONE WITH THE DIVINE

*Not every bubble affects every person, but every bubble can affect those people whose thoughts are linked to any given bubble.*

## Divine Love to the Rescue

Humans have been led to believe that they have little to no ability to change the world unless they are in a position of absolute power. A comment about quadraquippy bubbles may cause the average person to experience mental overload.

Here is the truth:

*All mankind can interact with the mass consciousness to change quadraquippy energy bubbles. We utilize Divine Love Petitions designed for the highest good of all.*

If a belief system is spiritually correct, then that mass consciousness quadraquippy bubble can download a beneficial effect to all humans. The *spiritual essence* of each human being can differentiate those bubbles that represent the spiritual truth. Thus, each person can accept or reject the beneficial effect of a bubble.

## Correcting Mass Consciousness

The Creator has given mankind *free will*. Thus, you can make choices and believe whatever you want to in life.

*What you choose to believe about any particular topic is not necessarily the spiritual truth.*

If you ask your *internal spirit* to guide you, you will quickly access and be able to understand whatever spiritual truths there are in any mass consciousness bubble you encounter.

What does the above paragraph mean to you since so many confused and even evil thoughts are constantly being generated?

Moreover, how can you be sure that it IS the spiritual truth being revealed to you?

Obviously, something important must happen for you to recognize the spiritual truth. What is it?

*You must make a leap of FAITH from what you believe today to what your internal spirit is trying to teach you.*

This *spiritual education* can be a very difficult transition. Many people are afraid of spiritual

# BEING AT ONE WITH THE DIVINE

contacts, the Creator, or believe they may need to give up something to which they are strongly attached. Surely there must be a better way to help millions of people!

*What we CAN do is join together with spiritual intention and apply that joint intention to the mass consciousness to effect change.*

After years of spiritual healing research, we made the following very important discovery:

*When a group of people join together with their intention, but work with their* **minds** *to create change, that change may be implemented on a partial basis, or not at all, depending upon the accumulated strength of resistance in the quadraquippy bubble!*

*However, when that same group combines its spiritual essence with angels and then focuses on the mass consciousness bubble with a Divine Love petition to reveal spiritual truth, change really occurs. Sometimes the change is instantaneous; in other cases, the change appears to be a normal progression.*

## Correcting Mass Consciousness

The revelation:

*Making a change in mass consciousness does not take millions of people to counteract the billions of people who are producing or manipulating quadraquippy thought bubbles!*

The above is a very strong statement that needs to be explained. If one thinks of mass consciousness in terms of the media, e.g., radio, TV, websites, and newspapers, you can readily understand how easily people may be influenced if they believe whatever they see or hear. Or perhaps you think you could never make a difference in the mass consciousness because thousands of people are constantly trying to influence you, promoting their own points of view.

*The good news is that all spiritual truths remain true. What we are all doing is opening ourselves to the choice to know spiritual truth, whatever it may be.*

# BEING AT ONE WITH THE DIVINE

Most of the time, people are interested in producing a singular effect, such as bringing peace, stopping a storm, protecting against radiation, or some other tangible request. Sometimes, that *perceived need* is simply a doorway concealing the spiritual truth. Once the doorway is opened and the spiritual truth is revealed, the need for the symptom is no longer required and the energy of Divine Love rapidly heals the problem.

*In addition, humanity becomes spiritually aware of all the truths associated with a given bubble.*

*Then we all take a giant step forward together in consciousness, as human and spiritual consciousness become ONE with the Creator.*

Today you have a tremendous opportunity to participate with other people to change the mass consciousness, provided that it is done with Divine Love and your spirit. And, provided that your spiritual intention is for the highest good for mankind and the planet!

## Correcting Mass Consciousness

*What has just been presented may not be within your present belief system; you may need time to digest the information. But remember: We have been teaching these concepts since 2004 and they work!*

*If we want to change something in the mass consciousness, it is achievable with simple healing petitions.  All it takes is a handful of people who are willing to serve humanity and who are willing to be At One with the Divine.*

If group volunteers want to take on a major issue that affects every country on earth, then the group energy needs to be much higher or it may take much longer to implement a solution. Some of the topics that we undertook in the past were very difficult and required a lot more energy then was afforded by our small group.

## Get the Right Participants

What we would like you to understand is what happened when we took on very complex mass consciousness topics that required much higher energy than our groups could generate.  The average size group for our mass consciousness webinars was between 40 and 50 people.

# BEING AT ONE WITH THE DIVINE

*On some difficult topics, it would take multiple one-hour sessions to cover just ONE country! While our dedicated group of volunteers was very patient, it was obvious that we were not making substantial progress.*

I had been reluctant to pursue angelic help because we wanted people to understand that they were responsible for making changes in themselves and the world. When I asked the angelic kingdom and my Guardian Angel for help, I was told by them that they would help us whenever we asked. And ASK we did!

The very next meeting we were able to divide countries of the world into ten geographical areas and implement all ten areas within one hour!

*While you may not understand the full significance of this event, those of us on the program felt that it was miraculous.*

Today and for the rest of my life, I would not consider doing any healing work without the full support and participation of the angelic kingdom!

# Correcting Mass Consciousness

It is foolish to think that the problems of the world can be solved by mankind alone. We humans have done a poor job of preserving life, liberty, health and the earth.

*Fortunately, with angelic help, we can reverse destructive patterns.*

Some people have already chosen to form groups for healing work. We commend you all for your dedication and effort in providing an important function to help people.

Should you be interested in how we partitioned the world for Mass Consciousness work, here are the groupings that we used: Europe & the U.K.; Russia; China; India; all other Asia; South America; Africa; Australia & New Zealand; U.S., Canada, Mexico & Central America; Every Island Nation.

We have together developed a path of action and tested it. The Mass Consciousness healing Petitions work! Share your knowledge with others!

# BEING AT ONE WITH THE DIVINE

## Accepting the Reality

Newcomers to our website and to Divine Love spiritual healing often ask the same question:

*"Is this real? How can I be sure it will work for me?"*

The largest impediment to acceptance is the notion that things must happen according to the current beliefs of an individual. The reality is that energetic change does occur when done correctly, regardless of belief systems.

For those of you who want evidence of mass consciousness healing, please contemplate the following:

### Fukushima Incident

In March 2011, the nuclear reactor accident at the Fukushima I Nuclear Power Plant in Japan resulted in nuclear meltdowns and the release of radioactive material. More than 500 people from 19 countries joined us on a live mass consciousness webinar.

*Together, we did a Divine Love petition to raise awareness about taking proper precautions to protect nuclear plants against disasters. We also did a Divine*

# Correcting Mass Consciousness

*Love Petition to protect the people and all life forms in Japan from radiation damage according to Divine will.*

Almost everyone on the webinar felt a huge energy surge that lasted for several minutes.

There were definite results:

1. Several countries indicated that they would no longer operate reactors based upon the Fukushima design.   Also, several countries have shut down their reactors.

2. First responders to the Fukushima disaster were reportedly exposed to lethal dosages of radiation.  They should have died within weeks from radiation damage based upon exposure, as did the first responders in the April 1986 Chernobyl disaster.

One year later, the Wall Street Journal reported in a half page article that, to date, not one person in Japan had died from radiation exposure resulting from the meltdown. *This is a huge revelation because what physically happened to the people is contrary to the expected radiation damage.*

# BEING AT ONE WITH THE DIVINE

Also, there were reports from professional investigators that radiation did find its way into the sea, seafood, milk and other products that were consumed. Again, the Japanese people were protected despite radiation levels.

The casual observer might think that the reactor radiation damage must not have been very dangerous, but that is not true.

The good news is that the Japanese people were and apparently continue to be protected.

We do not claim to take full credit for this happening as we are sure that other well-intentioned groups throughout the world also contributed.

We believe that the Creator's Divine Love protected and continues to protect the people and all living matter. This is quite interesting, considering that the radiation level is still high.

## Hurricane Katrina

Following Hurricane Katrina in August 2005 there was concern in New Orleans that Lake Pontchartrain would overflow and flood the city. Pollution from Lake Pontchartrain and the

# Correcting Mass Consciousness

Mississippi River is well documented. A major health concern was that anyone coming into prolonged contact with the water could develop serious illnesses.

Just hours prior to the flooding, our mass consciousness group met and implemented, with the angels, a petition to protect the people of New Orleans from waterborne viral and bacterial contamination resulting from the storm. To our knowledge there was no outbreak of any serious waterborne illness. Again, it is very likely that other groups did the same thing.

These are but two mass consciousness topics that we have engaged in, but this work is not about who gets the credit. It is about acting as a unified group of people to implement Divine Love petitions, in conjunction with angelic help, to serve our fellow man.

There are many groups trying to serve humanity and the earth that are operating from a *mental* thought position. It is my experience that such activities are less effective than working with *internal spirit* in group work utilizing Divine Love Petitions.

# BEING AT ONE WITH THE DIVINE

*Do not blindly accept these controversial comments because they are being said here. Test the concepts for yourself. Find your spiritual truth and rejoice in that truth.*

## How to Change Mass Consciousness

The first step is to unify the participating group. We do that by having everyone draw in their breath and state the following Petition **aloud** and together:

**"With my spirit and Divine Love we connect together with the angels in service to humanity and the earth."**

Then we all pulse our breath to send the Petition to the mass consciousness. Then together we experience the increase in group energy. It is always a profound spiritual event with many gifted people reporting on the energy changes that they are observing in the world.

Usually we spend about twenty minutes reviewing the webinar topic so that everyone has a good understanding of the topic and why we are doing the mass consciousness petitions.

# Correcting Mass Consciousness

Next we implement two different Petitions:

## 1. Worldwide Divine Love Awareness Petition.

The presenter asks everyone to read the Petition aloud. When done, we draw in breath and pulse breath to release the Petition to the mass consciousness.

> *"With our internal spirit, and with the Creator's angels, we send our combined Divine Love to the Mass Consciousness.  Our intention is to dissolve immediately* (state intention). *We ask that the Creator give all people a correct understanding of* (state the intention) *according to the Creator's will."*

We allow about 10 minutes for this petition to settle into the mass consciousness.  Then we turn the petition over to the angels to finish energizing and implementing the petition.

In September 2013 we presented a webinar on drug and alcohol addiction.  This first Petition was implemented as shown on the next page. The bold text is standard content and the normal text is unique to the topic of the day.

# BEING AT ONE WITH THE DIVINE

*"With our internal spirit, and with the Creator's angels, we send our combined Divine Love to the Mass Consciousness. Our intention is to dissolve immediately,* human disregard for the dangers of alcohol and drug abuse. *We ask that the Creator give all people a correct understanding of* the dangers of alcohol and drug abuse, all done *according to the Creator's will."*

Again, we share the experience with each other because many people with spiritual gifts report on what they sense is happening. Frequently, attendees see massive swirls of energy and colors wherever they are in the world. It is always exciting to hear and share attendee live-action reports with the entire group.

## 2. Worldwide Divine Love Healing Petition

Next, we address the appropriate Healing Petition for the topic of the day. In this petition we always ask that the spirit of every living man, woman, and child on the planet join with us in this petition. Since we are all spiritual brothers and sisters, including everyone raises the energy of the Petition considerably.

## Correcting Mass Consciousness

We always ask that the spirit of every living man, woman, and child on the planet join with us in this petition. Since we are all spiritual brothers and sisters, including everyone raises the energy of the Petition considerably.

Also note that we are ASKING the Creator to make the corrections with Divine Love and according to the Creator's will. We do this so that we do not inadvertently interfere with the Divine Plan of the Creator.

Here is the general petition that is used:

> *"With our internal spirit, together with the Creator's angels, we send our combined Divine Love to the spirit of every man, woman, and child on the planet. We ask that the Spirit of every living person join with us in this Petition. We ask the Creator to (state intention), according to the Creator's will."*

As an example, please see the next page for the actual Petition used during the drug and alcohol addiction webinar.

# BEING AT ONE WITH THE DIVINE

*"With our internal spirit, together with the Creator's angels, we send our combined Divine Love to the spirit of every man, woman, and child on the planet. We ask that the Spirit of every living person join with us in this Petition. We ask the Creator to* remove the need for drug and alcohol abuse in all people and to heal their systems without withdrawal symptoms, *according to the Creator's will."*

Again, we wait for about ten minutes for the Petition to complete or we turn it over to the angels to finish the implementation. We also discuss experiences and ask people to keep watch carefully for changes to occur.

## Timing Mechanisms

We are always asked, "When and for whom do the Petitions create change?"

Remember that people have free will.

This means that some people are open to positive actions and spiritual truth and others are not.

## Correcting Mass Consciousness

The Worldwide Divine Love Awareness Petition quadraquippy bubble component that is *untrue* discharges in a finite time that can be instantaneous or extended, according to the Creator's will. The spiritual truth then enters the consciousness of those spiritual people who are ready to perceive the truth.

In like manner, the Worldwide Divine Love Healing Petition begins to act on people as soon as the Worldwide Divine Love Awareness Petition has completed. Again, any person can reject the effects of the Petition with their free will.

*Once the desired conditions are set in the Mass Consciousness by using the group Worldwide Divine Love Awareness Petition and the Mass Consciousness Worldwide Divine Love Healing Petition, anyone is able to access the Divine Love contained in the bubble.*

**Then, as human beings choose to change their lives, that change can be accomplished rapidly with a very simple petition that will be presented in Chapter 10.**

*It is a miracle that curiosity survives formal education.*

~ *Albert Einstein*

# Chapter 5

# Divine Love Healing
# and
# Health Practitioners

**Just as a candle cannot burn without fire, men cannot live without a spiritual life.**

~ Buddha

# The Revolt

In many parts of the world, the general public has turned against organized medicine for a variety of reasons. Alternative Medicine is now more readily available and accepted.

Unfortunately, whenever a new modality presents itself, many people use the same language to expand therapies that might not otherwise gain public acceptance. This is not the case with Divine Love Healing because it has proven itself over many years.

## Understanding the Unseen Miracle

From 1985 to 2009, the healing petitions that we originally developed and reported upon in my book, SURVIVING CHAOS: HEALING WITH DIVINE LOVE reached the general public via workshops and a published training course.

People got amazingly fast results because the energy levels of the assembled groups were phenomenally high. When done properly the healings that were provided were complete.

In cases such as heart disease or lung cancer, it took 5 to 10 days for a recipient's cells to respond and to be completely healed. In all cases, we asked people to continue taking their prescribed medicines and to approach their physicians in 10 days for testing to confirm their recovery.

## Client Responses

Some clients approached Divine Love Healing without any hesitation. Other clients struggled with the fear of what their physicians might think or do after the healing.

Clients would be told by their doctors that their cancers had inexplicably gone into rapid remission. Sadly, patients seldom confided in their physicians that they had experienced a Divine Love Healing.

Even with that knowledge, physicians would usually not alter treatment plans. As a result, a patient would stay on chemotherapy for an indefinite period "to make sure" the cancer was gone.

This omission of communication and lack of understanding usually produced three results:

# Divine Love Healing and Health Practitioners

1. The omissions did little to help the physicians' understanding and added unnecessary stress to patient systems.

2. There was confusion in hospitals when ill patients suddenly recovered and when certified lab tests confirmed this. Sadly, physicians generally made excuses for the results and claimed test errors.

3. In other cases, records mysteriously disappeared from hospitals and physicians argued amongst themselves, frequently claiming that a wrong diagnosis must have originally been made.

At one time we attempted to collect legitimate hospital records to certify healings, but soon learned that this was unachievable.

We completely understood the denial and tendency to claim that whatever happened was a miracle, even when people knew we were simply working with the forces of the Divine.

I find it amazing that people subject themselves to being poked, prodded, and medicated, often until they are barely functioning, instead of first turning to Divine Love Healing.

## Volunteer Responses

When volunteers were present during a group healing and witnessed rapid recoveries, this reinforced the belief that this type of healing is real. As they told their friends, the acceptance of Divine Love Healing increased.

## Physician Responses

Over the years, many physicians have been willing to openly examine the results we were getting. Yet many of these same physicians have feared to openly support Divine Love energy healing for four reasons:

**1. It may be contrary to their training.** Some were afraid to take a public stand for fear of being ridiculed by their colleagues. On the bright side, some medical schools today are beginning to teach that spiritual factors may enter into healing work. As a result, some new doctors are more open to Divine Love energy medicine and some medical schools are offering classes on human energy.

**2. Physicians do not want to be sued for malpractice.** Despite results, few champions came forward from the health care ranks.

# Divine Love Healing and Health Practitioners

**3. A few physicians considered spiritual healing a threat to their livelihood.** After all, if a patient can be healed in a few days, where does the physician find a replacement patient?

Although there is generally a shortage of good physicians except in major cities, they should realize that more people can be helped at lower costs.

**4. Who gets paid?** During a writing workshop with Mark Victor Hanson years ago, I asked him how to present an introduction of Divine Love Healing to people.

Mark responded by asking, "How do you sell Divine Love?" Of course you don't, and therein lies the problem for the healthcare industry. We cannot sell someone what they already possess in abundance:  Divine Love.

What we can do is teach people how to work with Divine Love effectively in all aspects of their lives.  This  can be done in collaboration with other wellness programs for which the healthcare professionals can be reasonably compensated.  For example, much of our population needs some kind of counseling, e.g., dietary, spiritual or psychological, in addition to conventional medical tools.

## BEING AT ONE WITH THE DIVINE

Divine Love Healing can correct many health problems, but the successful client must change behavior to maintain health. This may include managing food, drink, and chemical intake, or the elimination of risky life practices.

## Teaming Possibilities

I will always look forward to working with physicians.

*My hope for the future is for a **combined effort,** with patient, doctor, and a spiritual healing facilitator, all working together.*

Once patients and doctors understand that they can achieve healing results, the term "miracle" is replaced by the expectation that Divine Love healing can be integrated into a healing team model.

Better coordination between modern medicine and spiritual healing work will result from this "healing team" concept. This is a win-win situation because:

*The patient feels more comfortable due to his increased participation and improved understanding.*

## Divine Love Healing and Health Practitioners

*The doctor has a facilitator who can help identify how to heal a resistant problem with Divine Love.*

*The Divine Love facilitator helps educate doctor and patient in the use of the Divine Love Healing process.*

Such a team effort will allow:

More clients to be seen.

Many troublesome side-effects to be eliminated.

Equal healing opportunities for people in remote areas and for those who do not have sufficient medical insurance.

Potential healing solutions for illnesses that do not respond to conventional medicine.

We are now at a transition point, where instead of conflict between healing modalities, we can all benefit by working together to apply the principles of Divine Love in every aspect of conventional and alternative medicine.

## BEING AT ONE WITH THE DIVINE

We define spiritual healing as the recognition of God, the Creator of the universe, and the Creator's energy that we call Divine Love. Many cultures believe that the Creator has bestowed energy upon people through a Holy Spirit. To me, that Spirit is Divine Love.

**I have just three things to teach: simplicity, patience, compassion. These three are your greatest treasures. Simple in actions and in thoughts, you return to the source of being. Patient with both friends and enemies, you accord with the way things are. Compassionate toward yourself, you reconcile all beings in the world.**

*~ Lao Tzu*

# Chapter 6

# Transitions

**Fear is the main source of superstition, and one of the main sources of cruelty. To conquer fear is the beginning of wisdom.**

~ Bertrand Russell

# Make Informed Decisions

Before we delve into the latest techniques for Divine Love healing, please think about the importance of your making informed decisions.

Considering the multitude of choices available from the alternative energy marketplace, many people are too quick to try a Divine Love healing technique, without understanding or appreciating the Divine gift that is being offered to them by the Creator. There are also "educators" who refuse to believe anything unless it conforms to their world view or supports their objectives.

*You must learn to think for yourself and depend on your internal spirit to lead you.*

To further complicate matters, it seems as if every new teacher adds new definitions and terminology in order to promote his latest offerings. Following are four ways to help you determine if you want to spend your time and resources to learn about a new topic:

*1. Look at the results.*

*2. Verify that teachings use Divine Love.*

BEING AT ONE WITH THE DIVINE

*3. Be sure your teacher is empowering you to seek out spiritual truth and is not just promoting a program.*

*4. Avoid modalities where personal love is used in the healing work because that may slow your healing. If you don't know whether your provider is using personal love or Divine Love, ask.*

## Today's Alternative Energy Market

Currently, there is activity by scientists and entrepreneurs to develop alternative medical devices as well as free energy devices. Some of this work is to be applauded and some of it may be dangerous for the novice.

There are some who suggest that mankind has all the answers through new technology, but that is simply not true! There are ancient energy technology systems which surpass what we have today! We will explore one such system together.

Once you finish this book, you will know the truth and you will be able to continue your knowledge quest in a safe manner utilizing your personal inner guidance.

## Transitions

Remember that you can confirm the reality and success that people have had with our healing systems by examining the case histories on the main page of our website. No gadgets, crystals or electronic devices were used to produce the results reported. . . just Divine Love Healing.

## Healing Miracles

During Divine Love group work, observers often commented, *"Look what they just did: They performed a miracle."*

What people actually observed were *natural events.* In fact, once you have learned the fundamentals and apply Divine Love healing in your own life, you will realize that you have facilitated your own *personal miracle.*

## Wake Up

It is time for people to awaken to the realization that they are *not limited* in what they can achieve energetically. Individuals can now experience true healing by operating alone. We will now focus on a Divine Love Healing system that does *not* require group participation.

# BEING AT ONE WITH THE DIVINE

*Be assured that there is sufficient Divine Love energy available to meet all your needs with or without a group.*

## World Service Institute Healing Systems

We are about to discuss our current healing systems in depth.  Over the years our Process has been updated and simplified as we learned more about how the human body heals.  Today World Service Institute offers two healing programs:

*1.* An on-line **Divine Love Free Healing Program** that we support 24 hours a day.

2. A fee based "how to" spiritual *self-healing process* taught via computer webinars.  This process reaches our worldwide audience through our highly acclaimed main teaching platform, the *Healing Yourself From Within Webinar* series.

Transitions

# Enter the Self-Healing Model

In 2010, we became aware that the energy of Divine Love had started to increase. We began to introduce some individuals to a different way of achieving a spiritual healing. We still used Divine Love, but we were trying to show students that they were able to work directly with Divine energies to affect their own healing *without a group.*

The new technique worked well for minor injuries and uncomplicated emotional releases, but the results were sporadic until mid-2010 for all other applications. Some students could simply *not* process Divine Love in their bodies at levels high enough to break through major diseases working alone.

We observed in the second half of 2010 that the energy of Divine Love was increasing rapidly and that people were further enabled to effect change in themselves! However, the results were still not substantial enough to warrant teaching the general public the self-healing technique that we were developing.

The energy continued to increase until October 2012 when the energy of Divine Love stabilized at a new higher vibration (frequency).

# BEING AT ONE WITH THE DIVINE

We were excited for our students because suddenly they were starting to get the results that they had been striving for!

We waited until December 2012 to introduce the new self-healing technique to the general public in our first *Healing Yourself From Within Webinar.*

*The Result: Immediate and simultaneous healings occurred in webinar attendees all over the world!*

## Effect Of Dimensional Vibrations

Following the December 2012 webinar, we realized that some people still had uncorrected symptoms; those symptoms were caused by very high energy interference patterns that had not been addressed in the webinar. We call these *"Dimensional Vibrations."*

Most people were previously unaware of *Dimensional Vibrations.* Even their internal spirit could not access these vibrations; the use of our generic petition did not solve the problem.

*Dimensional Vibrations account for rather significant energy patterns that cause misalignments in our subtle energy fields and in our DNA, eventually manifesting as complex physical symptoms.*

*Usually the pattern causes a torquing of the energy fields in the human body. Visualize the top half of a vertical rope being turned clockwise while the bottom half is turned counterclockwise. That rope is the client's subtle energy system being affected by Dimensional Vibrations. This torquing can cause great pain in many clients.*

In January 2013, we again presented the *Healing Yourself From Within Webinar* series, including the *Dimensional Vibration Petition* for the first time.

People attained wonderful results! Releasing Dimensional Vibrations facilitated additional instantaneous healings. Chronic pain and suffering symptoms were gone!

*Most of the people on the Healing Yourself webinars achieved self-healing, all without group support. (All of the healing reports on our website are written by attendees in their own words.)*

## BEING AT ONE WITH THE DIVINE

The Divine Love energy increase has definitely become a "game changer." Individuals now have a proven method to learn self-healing for themselves.

## Good Grief!  I Have a Pimple

Most everyone has looked into the mirror to discover a pimple. That pimple is a metaphor for what can happen with the increase in frequency of Divine Love:

1. Issues that people may have suppressed in their subconscious for many years are now manifesting suddenly: the outbreak of disease, pain, emotional distress, etc.  (The pimple has appeared!)

2. Issues and their symptoms are becoming so strong that people can no longer ignore dealing with them.  (The pimple keeps growing until we recognize that we must take action and correct it.)

Fortunately, we can all learn to use the Divine Love Healing Process taught in our *Healing Yourself From Within Webinars* to release and heal most of these troublesome issues.

## Transitions

People all have different experiences. Some people can use a Petition once with astounding results; others go through a learning curve as they build *trust* in the healing process and learn to confront and release their symptoms.

Later we will demonstrate how to use these Petitions correctly, but first we need to deepen your understanding about preconditions.

## The Spiritual Preconditions

With high frequency Divine Love, we noticed that significant *spiritual conditions* come to the surface.

For example, when a few webinar attendees tried to use the Petitions, they did not get results. That is because these individuals needed to look more deeply within themselves to identify the true *spiritual root causes of their symptoms*. This is not a regression from large group healing results; large groups now have the same problem.

What is happening is that we are being given an opportunity to recognize and address our life issues and take immediate corrective action.

# BEING AT ONE WITH THE DIVINE

*If people seek healing for their problems, they can usually improve their health, but they must come to the Creator with a willingness to change.*

In my experience, people who deny a healing opportunity may continue to experience an increase in severity of their symptoms.

## Surrendering Your Life to the Divine

The frustration of not achieving a desired result often causes attendees to believe they must be doing a Petition incorrectly, or that the Creator is punishing them. Neither of those thoughts is true.

What is true is that it is often a problem of *TRUST*. People want to be in control, so releasing or surrendering to the Creator's guidance is not easily done. It may be hard for them to trust God the Creator, and yet, these same people want the Creator to heal them. An interesting paradox, isn't it?

In 2013, we observed clients who did not build a trusting relationship with the Divine. They incorrectly believed they could be in control of their health recovery; they could not and thus continue to suffer. It is not my intent to scare you, but it **is** my intent to awaken you spiritually!

I spoke with several webinar attendees who became frustrated when their stated symptoms were not immediately satisfied, especially when they heard live webinar reports of instantaneous healings in other attendees. What we know is that:

**1. A *person's individual spirit will always correct an unrecognized, yet life-threatening health problem first.***

*The major health problem is always resolved before spirit addresses a client-specified symptom. Thus, the individual's symptom becomes secondary compared to a major problem that may not even be presenting as a symptom yet.*

**2. Sometimes nothing happens when the Creator wants an individual to recognize and release a deeper issue that has compromised the individual's wellness** *(a spiritual pimple.)*

# BEING AT ONE WITH THE DIVINE

*This situation may be more difficult to recognize if you are not spiritually awake. Since you may NOT know the root cause, it is best to surrender ALL the root causes and all the incidents associated with those root causes to the Creator.*

*This is an act of surrender to the Divine.*

*If it is important for you to know what the root cause is, the Creator will make it known to you as it is released.*

The Bottom Line:

*Trust that the Creator will guide you to a solution.*


## Responding to Difficult Symptoms

From January through July 2013, we ran additional live broadcasts of the *Healing Yourself From Within Webinars*. Each webinar series was improved to include corrections for issues that frustrated  healing for slow-to-heal people.

These corrections are presented in the Appendix, so that you can see for yourself how to modify a petition to fit your own needs.

## Transitions

We suggest that you wait until you finish this book before exploring the Appendix because this healing journey is about to become even more profound!

In the following chapter, we will examine some incredible Divine Love Petition results that show self-healing in an entirely different light from other healing systems.

**If you let go a little
you will have
a little happiness.
If you let go a lot
you will have
a lot of happiness.
If you let go completely
you will be free.**

~ Ajahn Chah

# BEING AT ONE WITH THE DIVINE

Two monks were once traveling together down a muddy road. A heavy rain was falling. Coming around the bend, they met a lovely girl in a silk kimono and sash, unable to cross the intersection. "Come on girl," said the first monk. Lifting her in his arms, he carried her over the mud.

The second monk did not speak again until that night when they reached a lodging temple. Then he could no longer constrain himself and said angrily: "We monks don't go near females. It is dangerous! How could you do that?"

"But brother," the first monk said. "I put the girl down and left her there hours ago."

"Why are you still carrying her?"

~ *Zen story*

# Chapter 7

# Healing Yourself from Within

# BEING AT ONE WITH THE DIVINE

## The Basics

As we delve into the mystery of Divine Love, we will closely examine why it is really a Divine energy, but for now I would like you to contemplate these thoughts:

*People who use our healing systems get good results once they understand that the Creator's Divine Love is unconditional, unemotional, and non-judgmental.*

*Divine Love is neutral until activated; then it provides exactly what a person needs energetically. This is the first revealed mystery of Divine Love.*

*Our healing system depends upon a clear intention. An intention is a statement of what you are trying to achieve. We call our Divine Love intention a "spiritual intention" because we work with our individual spiritual essence rather than our minds.*

*Our internal spirit is what activates Divine Love when we state a Petition aloud. This is the second revealed mystery of Divine Love.*

## Healing Yourself From Within

We teach people to use their Spirit and to concentrate on accepting Divine Love into their bodies while using a carefully worded Petition.

We teach in a worldwide marketplace where language issues may make it difficult to understand what we mean by the words we use. We receive requests to translate our teachings into other languages, but that represents a huge investment that we cannot afford to make.

Instead, we strive for consistency in the development of Petition wording. This helps assure that the spiritual intention of what we are doing is maintained.

*When we work from a spiritual level, a non-English speaking person may not understand our spoken words, **but his spirit does!***

*Therefore, we are able to transcend language because the spiritual message contained in Petitions is understood by the internal spirit of every Petition user. Divine Love is an instant translator to our individual spirit. This is the third revealed mystery of Divine Love.*

# BEING AT ONE WITH THE DIVINE

## Sign Me Up!

Becoming spiritual depends on your willingness to surrender control of your total system to your spirit.

However, becoming spiritual is like taking a flying lesson from someone you don't know; it can be uncomfortable to say the least! To give up control of what you think you are to your spiritual essence can be equally scary!

The thought of losing control to an unseen force frightens many who see the Creator as a supernatural Being who is all powerful. Many people have been taught to *fear* the Creator instead of to *love* the Creator.

So who will guide you through your life?

> *The truth is, your internal spirit will lead you to the correct solutions as you operate with Divine Love. This is the fourth revealed mystery of Divine Love.*
>
> *Your spirit is all knowing and your spirit is waiting for you to ask for help.*

## Healing Yourself From Within

*When your spirit senses that you are sincere, your Spirit can act very quickly on your behalf.*

Since the Creator does not judge or punish, we can release control to our internal Spirit and then work with our *Spirit* and *Divine Love,* trusting that our spirit will lead us to a solution.

# Testimonies

Some people on our webinars heal rapidly; others take more time.  Below is my friend Lee's experience.

In this report Lee learned two things: that Divine Love Healing does work, and that her Spirit CAN and WILL help her to break a previously uncontrolled eating disorder.

*"I have been a compulsive over-eater for my entire life. Food has always controlled my life. With more than 100 pounds to lose, I didn't think it would ever change, even though I spent most of that time trying to control my eating and lose weight.*

*"On one hand, I love candy and sweets.  They are fun, joy and always the biggest part of any*

# BEING AT ONE WITH THE DIVINE

*celebration for me. On the other hand, being overweight is miserable. I hate being fat, out of shape and missing out on fun and life. This conflict in my thinking has been my mental construct for as long as I can remember.*

*"For the last two years, I had been studying Divine Love with Bob Fritchie. I have had great results in reducing anxiety, fear and misery. But the weight didn't budge.*

*"I began reading a Course in Miracles. In the Course it says, 'If you have troubles or stress, in an area of your life, ask God to show you how to see the situation differently. Ask to see your problems like God sees them.' So I asked my Spirit, in a petition, to show me how God sees my problem of overeating.*

*"My Spirit showed me that it was repeated childhood traumas and that I needed Spirit's help to stop. I could not stop myself.*

*"So I asked my Spirit, in a petition, to stop me from eating candy. My pattern was to obsess about not eating candy until I would break down and eat candy until I felt sick. Then I would hate myself and feel awful because I was so weak.*

# Healing Yourself From Within

*"Several weeks went by. I just kept repeating the same petition each day.*

*"I STARTED TO FEEL HOPELESS. With petitions I had been able to experience miracles of behavior change and be so much happier. But how could I stop overeating?*

*"One morning I woke up and while still in bed, I heard a voice in my head say, 'I am an angel called by your Spirit to help you.' Wow, my Spirit sent me an angel!*

*"I thought, 'What can you do for me? How do I know you are here to help me?' The angel said, 'Divine beings only offer solutions and goodness. If you are ever told something that you know is wrong or scares you, then it is not a Divine being and don't listen to the advice.'*

*"The angel said to me, 'Raise your arm.'*

*"I raised my arm.*

*"Then the angel said to me, 'Now try to raise your arm again.' My arm would not move!*

*"How is this going to help me?, I asked the angel. The angel said, 'Go get some candy.'*

# BEING AT ONE WITH THE DIVINE

*"I went and got a package of Reese's Cups and opened them.* ***WHEN I TRIED TO MOVE MY ARM TO PUT THE CANDY IN MY MOUTH - MY ARM WOULD NOT MOVE. I COULD NOT EAT THE CANDY.*** *Trust me, I tried several times.*

*"The angel said, 'You are no longer going to eat sweets or candy. I am here to help you stop yourself.'*

*"Instead of being angry I felt so grateful. It was a blessing to finally have some control over myself.*

*"A new development has happened recently. No sweets appeal to me anymore. I don't have any emotion about candy or sweets.*

*"I asked the angel who was helping me what was happening and the angel said, 'I stopped you from eating candy until your Spirit could take the emotion out of your feelings for candy.'*

*"This is the middle of my eighth week of self-control. My Spirit tells me to be patient as it is going to take some time to change all my beliefs about food, exercise, and self-control.*

# Healing Yourself From Within

*"I'm a work in progress, but to know my Spirit can help me. I think that is amazing."*
*~ Lee, Ohio, U.S.*

This is an amazing testimony! Everyone who wants to can persevere and get results. Notice that Lee did not get an answer to her Petition until her spirit determined that she was totally sincere in her request and needed help from the Divine.

Now read this report from a man who was determined to correct heart disease. He found our website and used the *Divine Love Free Healing Program*. Here is what happened:

*"I want you to know that I suffered a **major heart attack on May 13, 2012** (never before having experienced any major challenge to my life and health.) **The doctors told me that I had 20% heart function and that it was likely that I would have permanent heart damage.** I somehow found your site online and did the 14 day healing (with my whole heart & soul.)*

*"Two months later an EKG and blood tests indicated **that my heart had been completely healed and that my heart function was normal.***

# BEING AT ONE WITH THE DIVINE

*"The doctors were amazed."*
*(ed note: R. reported later that his heart healed without scarring.)*
        *~ R., USA*
*(2012 Divine Love Free Healing Program)*

There are many such reports on our website from people all over the world.

One of my other favorite stories is from a woman in Australia who was addicted to alcohol.  Here is her report:

*"I am writing with some really good news at long last.  **The miracle has happened.  The alcohol addiction has healed and is gone.** I can feel it in my body.  The healing process has been so profound and beautiful and complete that it touches me somewhere very deep and it defies words.  It is a miracle.  This is what I experienced over the five days since your webinar:*

*"**Day One** - unusual tiredness, like lead in my blood stream.  At times, I battled to stay awake during the day.  There was a big energy coursing through me and about me.*

*"I followed your advice and just breathed deeply and let it all go. This worked really well.*

# Healing Yourself From Within

*But, I had to keep it up. I had mild irritability too.*

*"**Day Two** - I was much calmer and not tired. I was only mildly agitated at nightfall - the danger time. But, I told myself to trust and went within to discover avalanches of loving energy that seemed to be just sitting there with a warm smile. I relaxed into that feeling and all was well. In fact, I felt a wellness.*

*"**Day Three** - I experienced the joy of having long stretches of not even thinking about the problem - a quiet but beautiful relief after decades of being driven mad about the problem. I went for a swim and did my usual 30 lengths. During the meditation of the laps, I wondered if I was kidding myself that this could really (have) happened to me. My inner voice spoke very resolutely and told me to 'sustain the faith and accept the love.' I DECIDED then that I would. I developed a scary sugar craving and started eating the house down of sweets.*

*"**Day Four** - I felt a very powerful energy flowing about me and could almost see it at times in a diaphanous form. I trusted it with my heart. Felt great, except for the desire for sugar. I knew I was healed of the addiction.*

# BEING AT ONE WITH THE DIVINE

*"**Day Five** - Like a miracle, the sugar cravings lifted and fled my being. (This blew my head!!) I felt surges of energy in the crown area throughout the day, including strong systems of flashes of silver light. I felt great and very secure inside myself. I knew the addiction was gone intuitively and in my physical self.*

*"**Day Six** - I am writing this email to you and I feel a new peace and calm. I am healed. This is so profound. It ends a hell road of struggle and emotional pain. I am just so thrilled and elated.*

*"I thank God with all my heart and I thank you with all my heart. Thank you Bob for not letting go of my healing journey, particularly, when I have been such a wretchedly bad patient. You have been the difference. I love you so much."*
*~ A., Australia,*
*(2013 Releasing Emotional Imprints With Divine Love Webinar)*

We could fill several books with reports like these but what would be the point? You either get it or you do not!

And just what is it that you need to "get?"

# Healing Yourself From Within

*It is that when you work with your Spirit and Divine Love you are not limited in what you can achieve.*

Let's look at what has happened to a woman who took our webinars and then formed a Divine Love Healing group on the West Coast.

*"I first heard you in an interview with Cheryl Richardson. I was fascinated that you were able to use God's Divine Love as a source of power to heal people. I first started connecting to the Free Healing Program to pray for others.*

*"Then I gathered about 5 other people and we started connecting to the Free Healing Program to send God's Divine Healing Love to others. Last year I was able to attend a couple of your webinars and learned how to apply our Birthright and tap into the healing power within ourselves using the petitions. I have shared this with our group and we are seeing miraculous things happen.*

*"One woman who had cancer in her lungs, liver and brain - in 3 weeks is cancer free.*

*"Another woman who had kidney disease - no longer has any disease in her kidneys; one woman with scar tissue in her colon - when*

147

*they went in to remove the scar tissue it was dissolved and no longer there.*

*"One man who they were going to put on dialysis - no longer needs it and was not put on dialysis.*

*"One young man they said had cancer in his bones - test came back no cancer in his bone marrow.*

*"And one woman they said had cancer in her hip - results came back no cancer in her hip.*

*"I know there are nay-Sayers, but I have seen people miles away healed because a few people were faithful and willing to try and see lives changed by directing God's Divine Healing Love to others. Thank you again."*
~ DD, California, USA
(2012 Divine Love Free Healing Program)

## About Petitions

What then is the main component of Divine Love Healing and what makes it work?

## Healing Yourself From Within

Spiritual energy healing is very simple, but produces amazing results.

*All that is needed is for us to work with our internal spirit, together with Divine Love in a Petition that asks the Creator directly for help!*

Moreover, it is very clear that Divine Love spiritual healing has become a tool to be used, not only in the development of your spiritual awareness, but also in the recovery of your health.

# Past vs. Future

One day I became spiritually aware that what we have been teaching is not new. It is ancient and predates organized religion!

We will now delve into the *past* history of healing, so that I can help you to learn what you can do. We are going to trace the evolution of one of the ancient energy healing systems as it migrated around the world.

Divine Love healing has evolved in our time frame and is now operating on a very high spiritual vibration that has returned to the earth. This vibration is the same as that used by the ancient healing system that we will discuss in the following chapters.

Please try to read the next three chapters with an open mind.

**The greatest conflicts are not between two people, but between one person and himself.**

~ Garth Brooks

# Chapter 8

# Ancient Communication Systems

The important thing is not to stop questioning.  Curiosity has its own reason for existing.

One cannot help but be in awe when he contemplates the mysteries of eternity, of life, of the marvelous structure of reality.  It is enough if one tries merely to comprehend a little of this mystery every day.

Never lose a holy curiosity.

~ Albert Einstein

# Ancient Communication Systems

We'll begin with what we know about the past, then we will bring that knowledge forward into the present.

Many ancient healers were familiar with a variety of energy healing systems; some are still in use. Today we know that many of these systems appeared to have been developed in countries that had no knowledge of other countries. *BUT, is this really the spiritual truth? And if it is, then where did ancient people actually get their healing information?*

> *There must have been a system of learning that used the same basic principles.*

The energetic healing systems found in various countries are very similar. I don't believe this is a coincidence.

Archaeological excavations have revealed remains showing evidence of sophisticated cranial surgeries. How is that possible when there are no associated records of such procedures AND we are talking about remains that are thousands of years old?

# BEING AT ONE WITH THE DIVINE

## The Monuments

There are energy monuments scattered all over the world that were used to educate people, communicate without telephones, and provide healing energy. These systems were well known many thousands of years ago. Unfortunately, much of the information was concealed or lost in cataclysmic events.

Dr. John Sase has completed a monumental piece of research that traces ancient sacred sites around the world.

His book, CURIOUS ALIGNMENTS, THE GLOBAL ECONOMY SINCE 2500 B.C., is available through Amazon.

Dr. Sase had noticed that several sacred sites in the state of Michigan were seemingly connected when he superimposed geometric forms over the mapped sites. Dr. Sase asked me what I thought of his observations.

I suggested that he draw lines along the base sides of each geometric form that he was studying and extend those lines around the earth. John did this using Google Earth maps.

*What he found has staggering implications!*

154

# Ancient Communication Systems

*Dr. Sase confirmed that there is a grid of sacred ancient sites that are aligned with one another upon the earth!*

Some of these sites are well known to archaeologists. Sites are in France, the U.K., Egypt, Peru, India, Europe, Mexico, China, Persia, America, and on Easter Island in the Pacific Ocean.

The sites all had their own cultural evolution. It became evident to me that these sites must have shared much of the technology and spiritual connectivity that we see today.

Some of the sites were stone pyramids. When an extended line is drawn along the base onto a Google world map, the lines inevitably intersect with the baseline of other pyramid-like monuments. By observation it can be seen that all the sacred sites are indeed truly aligned to other sacred sites all over the earth!

This phenomenon cannot be a coincidence. It strongly suggests that the sites are all part of a master network that allowed communication between the early inhabitants of earth and whoever masterminded the grid design.

Many of these sites are in the form of rock pyramids. It is believed by other investigators that the pyramid base-edge alignment was necessary to improve the *pyramid energy reception*. This effect is similar to tuning a microwave antenna in today's technology.

Scientists are beginning to re-discover the real use of these sites. The rate of discovery will probably increase because there are people spiritually awakening now who have lived during those ancient times.

As people remember their spiritual birthright, they can apply the ancient teachings in today's world. It is my expectation that in a few years mankind will relearn this higher technology and once again experience life without pollution or illness.

## Where Healing Information Came From

How did advanced energy healing really begin? Evidence points to the continent of Mu, known to the ancients as the Motherland of the known world at that time. Mu flourished about 12,000 years ago in the Pacific Ocean.

Remember that I asked you to read the next two chapters with an open mind. Then ask yourself what resonates with you as spiritual truth.

# Mu Energy Systems

The ancient literature describes Mu as a lost continent in the Pacific Ocean. Descriptions of Mu and its culture are found in the temple archives of Tibet, India, Mexico, the Incas, the Mayans, Egypt and some American Indian tribes.

I first learned of Mu when still in high school. My father, who knew of my interest in archeology and all scientific things, gave me a book, THE LOST CONTINENT OF MU. The author was Colonel James Churchward, a British army officer who was recognized as a famous archaeologist and explorer in the late 1800's. The book was originally published in 1931 and went through 18 printings.

When Churchward was stationed in India, he met an Indian holy man who knew how to translate the ancient tablets in India's most sacred monasteries. The holy man taught Churchward how to decipher the tablets. Later, Churchward inspected nearly identical tablets in Mexico, Egypt, Burma and Tibet.

# BEING AT ONE WITH THE DIVINE

*The same messages appeared in all of the ancient tablets.*

*The tablets stated that educational and spiritual information was distributed to Polynesia, Mexico, India, Tibet, and the Mayas by teachers from Mu.*

*The tablets described Mu as the motherland of civilization with a mass population of about 12 million and that Mu was destroyed by a cataclysm that caused the continent to sink into the Pacific Ocean nearly 12,000 years ago!*

The destruction of the continent must have resulted in severe post traumatic stress for the few survivors who had lost their advanced civilization. Most of the survivors were the merchants and educators who had migrated along trade routes to other countries before the disaster.

When I first read the book, I realized that Churchward had done a great piece of scientific work. It was a major accomplishment to correlate information that had been found in other parts of the world, including the great pyramid of Egypt.

## Ancient Communication Systems

As expected, professionals in Churchward's time did not grasp the significance of his work because it did not fit their worldview of history. They tried to discredit his findings.

# The Structures

In Mu there were energy pyramids distributed across the continent from North to South. Each pyramid provided two distinctly different functions.

The First Function was for communication both on Mu and between Mu and other continents, utilizing a transmission technique that is now being re-discovered.  That technique was the storage of key information in *Information Stones*.

The Stones can be loosely compared to today's computer teaching systems wherein students can select and study topics on their computers.

In ancient days, both children and adults held the Information Stones between two hands, closed their eyes, drew in their breath and

# BEING AT ONE WITH THE DIVINE

extracted information energetically from the Information Stones. (Dr. Vogel showed me how to do this in 1980.)

The pyramids were purportedly operated by priests and priestesses who were also the spiritual leaders of Mu. It was their task to imprint the Information Stones with knowledge obtained through their spiritual meditations.

These pyramids were tuned, like today's microwave transmission systems, to move information from one energy pyramid to another. The people of Mu were thus educated by their spiritual leaders in all matters, including spirituality and science.

Mu teachers reportedly traveled to other continents and took the information technology with them to educate other cultures. That is probably why all the tablets examined by Churchward provided the same data.

The Second Function of the Mu Pyramids was to capture raw energy from the atmosphere and convert it to a useful form of energy for illumination.

Techniques for doing this are known today, but there are significant precautions that need to be put in place because the energy systems that were used then did not use AC or DC power. The energy can be destructive if not handled properly; today's power engineering design concepts for electricity do not apply to this technology.

If all this is true, what we are dealing with is a spiritual interaction between evolved spiritual human beings and advanced physical energy devices.

Now let's see what reportedly happened.

## The Destruction of Mu

Unfortunately, there was a serious design flaw in how raw energy was collected in the stone pyramids. Unused energy was incorrectly grounded to earth in the same manner that we ground electric circuits today. This incorrect grounding caused a buildup of energy that transduced into a large energy charge that increased over time.

Eventually, the "energy buildup" purportedly became too much for the earth, resulting in earthquakes, subterranean gas explosions and the eventual collapse and sinking of the continent.

The destruction of Mu seems quite plausible considering what today's scientists are dealing with, e.g., the large methane gas deposits trapped under melting ice in the Arctic Ocean. If the ice melts and the gas continues to escape, there is concern that there could be a massive explosion. Do you see the similarity of events?

## New Evidence of Mu

Physical evidence is coming to light. There is an underwater stone road off the coast of Japan that extends toward what is believed to be Mu; divers are amazed at the construction.

Off Okinawa, a huge submerged city, complete with pyramids, was discovered in 60 feet of sea water. It will be interesting to see if investigators retrieve tablets or information stones from the pyramids, as records were supposedly stored in all the pyramids.

# Viewpoint

I am not trying to build a case to support a theory. But when you consider what Dr. Sase discovered and what Colonel Churchward reported, it makes sense.

To acknowledge that information flowed much differently 12,000 years ago is reasonable to me when I think about how Divine Love energy has increased so quickly in just two years.

The spiritual truth will reveal itself. Think about this historical account, but do not be overly concerned by what the media reports, or what I have said.

*Instead simply ASK within yourself to know the spiritual truth.*

In the next chapter we will examine ancient healing systems.

**I never teach my pupils.**

**I only attempt
to provide the conditions
in which they can learn.**

~ Albert Einstein

# Chapter 9

# Relevance
# of
# Ancient Healing
# Systems

You are not a human being
in search of
a spiritual experience.

You are a spiritual being
immersed in
a human experience.

~ Pierre Teilhard de Chardin

# Relevance of Ancient Healing Systems

The healing knowledge developed in Mu reportedly gravitated to Indonesia in the Southwest, Chile to the East, Hawaii to the North, and to the Solomon Islands to the South. In each of these four locations, people learned to modify and apply a very simple healing solution that worked.

Teachers from Mu spread the information to Africa, America, Egypt and India. People in those locations in ancient times reportedly had very high energy and operated with a direct spiritual connection to the Creator.

As mankind evolved, people started to give this energy names and use it for different purposes. The Chinese masters called it chi, the Japanese called it ki, and the India Indians called it prana.

People today recognize that same energy but in an effort to be original call it "zero point energy," "universal energy," "source," etc.

I believe the energy should be respectfully acknowledged as the energy of God, the Creator of the universe. In our healing system we call that energy Divine Love.

BEING AT ONE WITH THE DIVINE

## The Lost Healing Art

Over time, populations lost their connections to this pristine healing system. Eventually, fundamental healing knowledge deteriorated, becoming the property of medicine men. For example, in Hawaii, the diminished healing system became known as Ho'oponopono.

## Return of the Lost Healing Art

We have introduced you to the ancient energy system that existed in Mu at a time when the universe and the people on earth were at a higher energy level and "At One" with Divine energy. This "At Oneness" enabled people to facilitate healing in themselves using the simple healing system in effect at that time.

We have explained how this ancient healing system propagated across the known world and survives today by many names in many countries of the world.

We will tie all this together in the next chapter.

# Chapter 10

# Into the Future

**I love you when you bow in your mosque, kneel in your temple, pray in your church. For you and I are sons of one religion, and it is the spirit.**

~ Khalil Gibran

# Into the Future

You have seen how the energy of Divine Love has been integrated into several of our healing programs. We started in 1985 with the Divine Love Group Healing Process and taught that for many years to large groups working together to serve a single client. In 2009, we adapted the DLGHP to use more descriptive petitions on Internet broadcasts to facilitate distant healing in individuals located throughout the world.

In 2013, we introduced a very powerful series of petitions that anyone can use to facilitate healing in themselves without group support. These are predicated on releasing and healing the "mental constructs" that block healing for webinar attendees. A mental construct is any closely held belief system that is not spiritually true.

The ability to facilitate individual healing has increased substantially among our webinar attendees. This has occurred because of the frequency increase of Divine Love.

## Divine Love Healing 2013

Until 2013 it was very difficult for human beings to accept the idea that they could facilitate their own healing using simple petitions. Many people have been taught since childhood that they are **separated** from God.

Also, as we grow older, we frequently develop and hold onto stringent and/or limited belief systems about life, spirituality and how the human body actually heals.

*We have shown conclusively that Divine Love energy healing is real and can be attained by people anywhere in the world in zero time.*

What we have not previously discussed is why some people are still resistant to healing. The original petitions provided in 2013 are listed in the Appendix so that you can see what people were struggling with at the time. The number one difficulty seems to be that some people no longer know what to believe in and trust, so they sit on the periphery of spiritual energy healing and do not fully engage. Many people are in a continuous mental battle as they strive to define what limits them. Surprisingly, their *religious beliefs* are *not* holding them back!

## Conflicted Thinking

There are  several conflicted thought processes in effect:

# Into the Future

**1. Definitions:** There is difficulty in agreeing upon the definition of key words such as "soul" and "spirit." (Spiritual people who accepted that their *internal spirit* controlled their healing were usually able to experience full healing.)

**2. Lack of trust:** Many believe that agnostics and atheists cannot use this healing process. That is incorrect; anyone who chooses to use the process can do so.

Now picture a small child testing his bath water by dipping his fingers or toes into it. The child wants a comfortable experience, so the water cannot be too hot or too cold.

If the child trusts the feeling from his fingers or toes as being a satisfactory temperature, he will readily enter the water, if only to have fun splashing. Thus children learn to develop and *trust* their own instincts.

The key for adults is similar:

> *We need to trust that the Divine Love healing process will lead us, the healing recipients, to a positive solution.*

# BEING AT ONE WITH THE DIVINE

During the healing experience, many *healing recipients* are given insight into the true spiritual nature of their existence. Our emails are filled with testimonies displaying a deeper understanding of what spirituality means to the healing recipients. Acceptance of spiritual truth is a choice, but not a requirement, for successful healing.

**3. *The energy of Divine Love:*** This is also a hurdle for many people. *Divine Love is a real energy field and it unites all people as ONE.*

"Love" means little to an abused or fearful person and may often translate into "*more punishment.*" Divine Love may translate into "*God is going to punish you!*"

Religious educators do not explain Divine Love as an energy field and simply say that "God is Love." *While true, it does not adequately teach how everyone can have access to and operate with Divine Love.*

Many religions do teach that there is a Divine energy in the universe, but it is often thought of as *symbolic* rather than *real* because it is not well understood. For example, the Bible refers to the Holy Spirit as the *enabling mechanism* that Christ offered to people to

174

# Into the Future

facilitate healing work. For some reason the message is not taught clearly.

*To me, the Holy Spirit is the same as Divine Love and is a sacred happening that occurs when someone activates the neutral energy of Divine Love with his or her internal spirit using a Petition to accomplish something.*

We are not religious teachers and you can accept or reject my viewpoint. What matters is that **Divine Love produces results**.

4. **Lack of a personal relationship with Divinity:** Many people believe in God as a Supreme Being, a high spiritual energy, or as the Creator of the universe. Yet many of these same people have *not* been taught that they can have a *direct personal relationship* with the Creator.

*Simply approach the Creator with humility and ask for spiritual guidance.*

*IF we can release all of the limitations and mental constructs that prevent us from being AT ONE with the Creator, we will, like the ancients, be able to use simpler healing systems.*

# What Illness Is

*Most illness is the result of an inhibited spiritual life.*

When we are able to release spiritual energy blocks, our cellular composition can rejuvenate and we can become well.  We have proven this repeatedly with group healing and individual self-healing using the two processes that we teach.

# Being at One with the Divine

In 2014 we will continue our webinar teaching series *Healing Yourself From Within* with new content and with new techniques.  At this juncture you may be satisfied with your healing progress and do not need more assistance. If so, you may elect to stay with the *Healing Yourself From Within Webinar* healing system introduced in 2013 that is presented in the Appendix.  There you will find the Petitions and instructions on how to use them.

However, if you are not healing, then our new **At Oneness Healing System** should be of help to you.

# Into the Future

To begin, let's examine this question:

*How do we transcend all of our limitations in working with the Divine in order to receive complete healing?*

The answer to this question is in two parts:

## 1. Achieve Oneness With The Creator

We must release forever the idea that we are separated from the Divine and the Creator for ANY reason.   And we need to be able to surrender ourselves completely to the Creator. When we do this, all our individual mental constructs and energetic blocks will dissolve, or can be quickly released when there is no longer any separation between us and the Creator!  We are **At One with the Divine**.

## At Oneness Petition

When you feel that you are ready to move forward and are sincere in your desire to achieve *Oneness with the Divine*, recite *aloud* the **At Oneness Petition** on the following page.

# BEING AT ONE WITH THE DIVINE

## The At Oneness Petition

*"With my spirit I focus Divine Love throughout my system. I surrender my entire being to the Creator. I ask my spirit to identify every situation and every cause that separates me from the Creator and release to the Creator all of those situations and causes. I ask that the Creator heal my system according to Divine will."*

This petition is the most powerful petition that I have ever worked with. It will completely clear you of any emotional traumas and mental resistance that you have in your relationship with the Creator.

*In effect, we become totally connected to the Creator.*

*There is no longer any self-imposed separation between us and the Creator.*

*You are spiritually home again, able to live your life in joy and peace.*

# Into the Future

## 2. Simplify Petition Wording

"Spirit" and "Divine Love" remain in our toolkit of petition words, but as we become AT ONE with the Creator, those words are spiritually understood. Thus, we no longer need to refer to them directly because all of us will be functioning as spiritual beings interacting directly with the energy field of Divine Love.

Since many emotional and other energy blocks are released and healed in the **At Oneness Petition**, it is possible to simplify further. Our existing *Unlovingness Petition* is unnecessary because unlovingness cannot coexist with *Oneness with the Creator.*

*In all future work we will use a simplified petition called the* **Lovingness Petition.**

Upon declaring that petition *aloud*, Divine Love will act upon the petition and the healing will complete more quickly. Some of you may be experiencing this effect right now.

*As people continue to engage with the Creator and ASK for help, most will experience a change in attitude about their spirituality and they will be able to achieve dramatic results.*

# BEING AT ONE WITH THE DIVINE

## The Lovingness Petition

There are several ways to use this new petition. I will give you the petition first and then explain how to use it.

**"I release my (name one symptom) to the Creator and ask that the condition be healed."**

Insert the name of any single symptom that you are trying to clear into the Lovingness Petition. Once people understand that *spirit* and *Divine Love* are inherent in the petition, they also understand why this short petition works. It is because we are *At One with the Creator, spiritually, mentally and physically.*

## The Missing Link

These two Petitions provide the missing link between the present vs. the ancient healing system described in previous chapters. That missing link is the title of this book:

BEING AT ONE WITH THE DIVINE

As we move forward in 2014 and beyond, our webinars will focus on demonstrating how to apply these two petitions more easily.

Into the Future

# New Petition Utilization

Do the **At Oneness Petition** first and wait until you no longer feel anything happening in your body. Then do the **Lovingness Petition** using **ONE symptom** that is spiritual, physical or emotional.

*Please avoid using a medical diagnosis.*

If you abide by the petitions that you use, then you will move forward. But if you believe that you can continue bad practices (drugs, alcohol abuse, unloving acts), you will find your healing progress is significantly restricted or halted.

If this happens, do the *At Oneness Petition* followed by the *Lovingness Petition*. Take note of your behavior and *use your behavior as the symptom in your Lovingness Petition*.


**If you continue to have a problem,
ASK the Creator for guidance and
follow through with what comes to you.**

## Staying Well

**When you use the two petitions, you must assume total and ongoing responsibility for yourself.**

The only thing that creates separation from now on is if you continue to act in an irresponsible or unloving manner. You will be made aware of this because your symptoms will reappear. If they do, repeat both petitions, but do the *At Oneness Petition* first.

You generally get what you ask for in a petition, provided that you are prepared to make changes in your life. This means that you may need to:

Learn how to develop a positive outlook.

Associate with other spiritual people who honor the Creator.

Avoid people who are not spiritual, who do not honor you as a person, or who choose to be negative. However, if you are in a situation where you must associate with someone like that, then send that person Divine Love. This action will break the restrictive pattern of behavior in both parties.

# Into the Future

Be willing to use the **Lovingness Healing Petition** as soon as a symptom manifests.

Learn about good nutrition.

Learn about chemicals and what not to allow in or on your body or in your environment. Learn about safe practices and incorporate whatever applies to you.

*Remember this:*

*Your Spirit controls your healing rate and it will not allow you to overstimulate your body by switching between petitions. Do ONE symptom in a petition until you get a definite result. A result should occur in 1 to 5 days.*

*If you do not get a result that you can detect in the first 5 days, then ask your spirit or the Creator for direction.*

*Treat your body as though you just had major surgery. Allow yourself recovery time to heal before doing a petition with a new symptom. Use the recovery times that follow as a guideline:*

## BEING AT ONE WITH THE DIVINE

*1. For emotional recovery, 2 days.*

*2. For addiction recovery, 5 days.*

*3. For sports injury recovery, 10 days.*

*4. For major disease recovery, 10 days.*

*5. For neurological problem recovery, 10 days.*

Repeat the **At Oneness Petition** followed by the **Lovingness Petition** as often, or as little as you like, but do **both** Petitions for every **new** symptom. Use these two petitions together about three times a day for the same symptom until that symptom has corrected.

## Your Future

This advanced *At Oneness Healing System* is fully functional right now! As we transition to this program we will all be At ONE in both spirit AND consciousness.

*After you have used this two-Petition process for the first time, you will be able to use the* **At Oneness Petition** *and the* *new **Lovingness Petition** for all future healing work for yourself or for others. Other Petitions are unnecessary.*

## Simplified Healing Techniques

### Chakra Healing

Everyone has seven main energy ports called *"chakras"* that distribute energy to key areas of the body. You can use the new *Lovingness Petition* as shown above to fine tune your system for faster healing.

**The technique described will clear your system; use the same symptom.**

For each chakra there is a portal on the front of the body and on the back of the body for chakras 2 through 6. The first chakra has a front portal and rear portal between the sex glands and the anus. The seventh chakra is located on top of the head, usually at the highest point, with the front portal closer to the forehead and the rear portal toward the back. The first and seventh chakras are oblong, with the two points of entry front and back, located at the narrow points of the chakra.

# BEING AT ONE WITH THE DIVINE

*The way to use the chakra clearing system is to focus with your Spirit and Divine Love **into each chakra,** starting with the first chakra, front side. You may be spiritually aware of the energy interfering with a chakra, but that is not required. Specify a **single symptom** and use the **Lovingness Petition** to release the symptom. Do so even if you cannot sense the presence of an energy block or imprint.*

***When energy stops moving in your body, ask the Creator if you should proceed to the second chakra; be sure to wait for an answer.** If there is no confirmation on a given chakra, wait and try again in a few hours.*

*When you receive a confirmation via telepathy or muscle testing, continue in like manner with each chakra.*

*Then start again with chakra number 1, backside, and move up through all seven chakras following the same protocol. Be sure to **ASK** the Creator about the advisability of moving to the next chakra before moving forward.*

# Into the Future

You will find that this is truly an amazing clearing technique because you do not need to know the content of each chakra. Notably, you avoid any unpleasantness from emotional releases that you might have using other modalities that do not utilize Divine Love.

*Obviously, if you have multiple illnesses you will want to proceed slowly. The sicker you are, the more patient you must be in allowing your body time to heal properly.*

Each chakra energetically feeds various organs and areas of the human body through the subtle energy fields. Please be sure that you have consent from the Creator before you address another chakra because each chakra contains significant keys to your health.

## Your Personal Healing

The concept of body balancing is inherent in doing the *At Oneness Petition*. You can use the *Chakra Balancing Petition* that is shown in the Appendix whenever you feel the need.

# BEING AT ONE WITH THE DIVINE

If a second (new) symptom appears (mental or physical) while you are healing, just use the *Lovingness Petition* **immediately** to release the second symptom.  If you do not get a complete release in five minutes, do the **At Oneness Petition** followed by a **Lovingness Petition** containing the second symptom.

*If you still have a problem, then ASK the Creator for guidance.*

## Proxy Healing

I've been asked many times about proxy healing but have hesitated to discuss this topic.

This is because most people who want to facilitate a proxy healing have very strong emotions of their own that cause them to link to the client.  Remember that your emotional involvement as a facilitator is to be avoided at all costs.

Once you have firmly locked into working with Divine Love and are getting results for yourself with these new petitions, then and only then, would I suggest that you participate as the facilitator in a proxy healing.

# Into the Future

A proxy healing is actually quite simple:   You ask that something be done for someone else who is unable, for any reason, to act for themselves.

A proxy healing must be done according to the will of the Creator and not your will because there may be a very good reason why the individual you are trying to help has the health condition that they are experiencing.   If you interfere before receiving authorization from the Creator to proceed, **you** may incur a significant energy debt that may affect your own health.

For example, let's say that you are trying to help "Sally."   If you know that you are operating unemotionally, and have asked the Creator for permission to proceed, and have received authorization to proceed, then use the petition below:

> *"I ask on behalf of Sally that she release the root causes of her (name the symptom) to the Creator and ask that the Creator heal her."*

There is another variation of proxy healing to use if the person you are helping is conscious, but cannot speak for any number of reasons.

# BEING AT ONE WITH THE DIVINE

Let's say that you intend to do a chakra healing on Sally. You should not use this approach unless Sally agrees to it before you begin.

*If Sally cannot give her permission do not proceed. Instead, ASK the Creator for guidance and act accordingly.*

*Sometimes an infirmity is given to help a client learn about her own spirituality; she should be encouraged to do the Petitions herself, silently.*

*Also remember to get the Creator's permission as you move from chakra to chakra so you do not stress Sally's body. You would use the Petition naming Sally, working through all her chakras, one at a time, starting on the front side of the body at chakra 1, then working to the top and restarting at chakra 1 on the back side.*

## Animal Healing

You do not need permission to heal animals, and they exhibit no resistance to healing. Therefore, you can work directly with a *Lovingness Petition* on any animal.

## Into the Future

Use the *Lovingness Petition* in the same manner that you would with a person. I like to put my hands on the animal that I am helping, but that is unnecessary.

We have also done large animal healing all over the world using distant healing. You can do so as well.

This year many birds have shown up for a healing, usually hopping about until they receive their healing using the *Lovingness Petition.*

Recently I found a delicate dragonfly that was obviously paralyzed by something. I put the dragonfly on my open palm and sent it Divine Love to heal it. In a few minutes, the dragonfly started flapping its wings and took off from my open palm. What a delight to watch such a beautiful creature recover!

A few days later I discovered a turtle in the yard. I sensed that he was quite ill and sent him Divine Love healing. Minutes later he left the area acting quite lively (for a turtle!)

# BEING AT ONE WITH THE DIVINE

## Mass Consciousness Healing

We have taught mass consciousness healing since 2009 and demonstrated it many times on significant incidents throughout the world. In the mass consciousness chapter, you learned how to change mass consciousness bubbles that are spiritually untrue.

You can make a major contribution by serving as a volunteer. Work with a group of people and combine your group energy to serve people, places, and things. I suggest that you continue to use the *Mass Consciousness Awareness Petition* and follow that with a *Mass Consciousness Healing Petition.*

## Nature Healings

Use the *Lovingness Petition* to heal any plant, whether tree, flower, fruit, or vegetable, that appears unwell. Before you do that, put your hand on the object, or hold a living leaf between your thumb and forefinger. Then ask if a healing should be done. You will feel a pulse in your fingers or your body if the answer is *yes*. Alternately, you can use the finger muscle testing as described in SURVIVING CHAOS: HEALING WITH DIVINE LOVE. If you do not receive confirmation do not proceed.

# Into the Future

You can correct a body of water such as a pond or small stream using a *Lovingness Petition* and the symptom of your choice. For larger bodies of water, such as lakes or rivers, work with a group of friends. Join your energy together with intention and then do the *Lovingness Petition* together. Pulse breath at the completion of the petition to send the petition to the intended subject.

If you are in an area with bad air, correct it with a *Lovingness Petition.*

## Negative Energy Correction

Public places such as offices, theaters, hospitals, airplanes, restaurants, and hotel rooms, as well as private structures such as houses, vehicles, apartments and enclosed boats often collect negative energy from the people who frequent them.

*Clear such areas and the people in those areas with a simple Lovingness Petition. Use "I send Divine Love into the (area) to clear it and the people with Divine Love."*

BEING AT ONE WITH THE DIVINE

## Food and Water Purification

If you are somewhere without clean food and water, do the *At Oneness Petition* first to make sure that you are totally connected to the Divine.

Then use a simplified *Lovingness Petition:* "I send Divine Love into the (target name) to purify and make it harmless." Pulse breath at the completion of the petition to send it to the subject.

One time I did not do this was on a trip a few years ago; somehow I contracted a bacterial infection, a foodborne illness. That was a miserable experience I could have avoided!

*It is good practice to purify everything that goes into your mouth before you consume it.*

## Energy Draw-downs

There is a concept that certain people act as *energy vampires.* The term is used to describe the condition you feel when you are near someone and feel energy suddenly leave your body. This is because that person is pulling energy from you.

### Into the Future

Describing people as *energy vampires* is both extremely unloving and discourteous to people in need.

*Instead of avoiding them, send Divine Love to help them.*

*They will charge up and feel better and you will also recharge!*

## Group Dynamics

In any group of people (public gathering, family, business, etc.) it is possible for negative energy to quickly accumulate.

*Simply pulse Divine Love to everyone as you enter the area to create a calm atmosphere.*

*Be careful NOT to include any other intention such as "getting people to agree with you." That is manipulation; you cannot use Divine Love selfishly.*

# BEING AT ONE WITH THE DIVINE

## Opening Up Communications

We all communicate with each other through our own **energy filters**. *Filters* contain our observations about people, for example, how someone smells, speaks, dresses, or expresses himself via mannerisms. These filters may cloud our understanding of others.

> *To clear filters, just send Divine Love to the individual or the group before you begin a conversation. That will clear their filters so that they can communicate clearly with you.*

> *Clear your own filters with the Lovingness Petition if you suspect that you have misunderstood someone else.*

We believe that everyone can benefit from applying the *At Oneness Petition and the Lovingness Petition* described in this Chapter. They eliminate the need for you to go through all of the Petitions that we offered during 2013, as given in the Appendix. The choice is yours.

# Into the Future

*We recommend that you attend the 2014 webinars where you will:*

*Learn the latest techniques, since new approaches will be added throughout the year.*

*Gain confidence in utilizing these Petitions correctly and gain a better understanding of our Divine Love Healing Process.*

# November 2013 Reports

## 1. Releasing Accident Pain

On her first para-sailing adventure, Laura crashed into a mountaintop with her instructor sitting behind her. She was badly injured with deep cuts and bruises on her legs. Laura did a Divine Love healing on her injured legs shortly after the incident and her leg injuries healed rapidly.

I did not know she was still hurting until I received the following report. This testimonial is the result of Laura doing the *At Oneness* and *Lovingness Petitions* on our November 2013 webinar.

# BEING AT ONE WITH THE DIVINE

"I said aloud the petitions during Tuesday night's webinar. I haven't done any other petitions/treatments since and am allowing the healing to happen. My symptom was pain in the legs - calves, heels, soles of the feet. The pains are gone - this is incredible.

"The healing since the accident has been incredibly fast. I am back at work (very physical - gardening) and in karate training since September. However, I have been awakened at night... with pains in the legs, and when putting on shoes and boots, the pain in both Achilles was very strong.

"I have not been awakened since Tuesday night; and am putting on shoes without pain, (tiny amount with boots on), but know that will leave too.

"I am in training 5 to 6 days a week and legs feel great. My doctor wanted me to have an MRI as she said there was severe cruciate ligament damage if not complete rupture back in August. I didn't have it, as my inner sense was one of consistent improvement, literally since the accident happened. That continues to be the case.

# Into the Future

"Thanks so much Bob for making this amazing information available. I have shared, and will continue to share with others. It's a pity some people don't seem to believe that healing could be this easy or fast!"
~ *Laura, Ireland*


## 2. Correcting an Old Health Condition

Anne has gone through a series of important healings. Her experience ties together many of the principles taught in this book.

"That was such a wonderful webinar last week and I thank you and God for it very much. You know, I think there was so much healing that happened. Much more than I am consciously aware of, I suspect.

"There was a beautiful mystery to it that was very loving and gentle, yet laser-like in focus. It felt as though Spirit picked up where we left off in September. Then, there was huge energy directed at my heart. Last Wednesday, it was my throat chakra, along the ridges of the crown of my head and just above my ears. It was so intense that I reported to you on the call about blurry vision and and a migraine-like headache. The clearing petition you suggested worked well.

# BEING AT ONE WITH THE DIVINE

"Everything continued through that petition and after that, although not as intensely. After the webinar, I felt the energy continue for a few more minutes, then a wave of joy came over me. I have not experienced that joy following a webinar. I had begun the call fatigued and ended it radiantly energized. There was a beautiful feeling of love within me and without. I felt centered and calm...and still do.

"I was perplexed by it all - given that my petition had referred to a lifetime bladder disorder which I am thrilled beyond measure to declare has now disappeared. I keep having to pinch myself about this, I really, really do.

"I have always been most embarrassed and disadvantaged by this condition. Having a cripplingly weak bladder blighted my life. I now have none of the pain or discomfort that would follow after taking in fluid. I have control and interestingly, I feel a peace in my bladder. I can actually feel it - peace. It feels like I am new. I am very close to tears in writing this to you because it is a wonderful gift and I am still very much coming to terms with the new experience.

## Into the Future

"I feel like I'm having a spiritual makeover! It wasn't until quite late the next day that I felt the shift in my bladder area...up until then it was all focused on the throat. I feel God has helped me to unchain from some very old burdens and is opening the way for me to give expression from my heart. I think there is an unfolding.

"The new petition is stunning in its speed and efficacy. Thank you so much for bringing it to us all and I can't wait for the webinars in 2014!"
~ Anne, Australia

## May you all
## live in peace
## and be
## At One with the Divine.

# Epilogue

Congratulations! Together we have covered 34 years of my spiritual journey. Those years and the years before my spiritual awakening were filled with many events that tested my perseverance and belief systems. It has definitely been worth my time and effort to travel my spiritual path. And hopefully my experiences will help to shorten your journey.

As you read through this book, you may have formed some new opinions. My hope is that you develop a close and trusting personal relationship with the Creator of the universe based upon Divine Love.

To work with our latest healing system effectively requires that you learn the basics concerning *spirit* and *Divine love.* Then you can decide for yourself if you are willing to commit to working as a *spiritual* human being in a mode that eliminates all concepts of

# Epilogue

*separation* from the Divine. In this book we have shown you how to begin that process.

Many people who came to us in the past believed that they could implement petitions mentally, without considering the importance of operating from *spirit* rather than *mind*. Those people did not have good results until they understood that all life is really driven by *spirit* and that we are all ONE in *spirit*.

*Once you grasp the principle that we are all ONE, then you also recognize that you can participate fully in changing the mass consciousness.*

It is through *Divine Love spiritual intention* that a group of people serving together can change the mass consciousness to improve the lives of all humanity. Because Divine love does not allow manipulation, changes to the mass consciousness can only reflect that which is for the highest good. You may want to form your own group to participate in this work.

The entire spiritual healing process of attaining *At Oneness* is similar to your discovery of a heavy wood door. You know that in passing through this door you will be *At One* with the Creator. But the door is locked and you have no key!

# BEING AT ONE WITH THE DIVINE

*However, as you learn to release those things in your life that you resist or are afraid of, you suddenly find that you are able to pass through!*

The door represents the resistance between life lived on a strictly physical basis, and a spiritual life where we are *At One* with the universe and the Creator.  This then is the ideal state to be in if we want to move forward.

*The advantage of "Being At One with the Divine" is that we can again experience true spiritual healing with two simple petitions that link us directly to the Creator via Divine Love.*

As you examine the Appendix, you will notice that you have a choice to use the petitions offered through December 2013.  These petitions represent a perfectly viable system that works!  If you do not get a result in a reasonable time frame, I suggest that you ASK the Creator for guidance.

Some of you will ASK for guidance and learn to pass through the wood door.  Those who do NOT ask, because they do not trust or may fear contact with the Divine, will not pass through their *self-imposed* wood door.

# Epilogue

We will continue the *Healing Yourself From Within Webinars* in 2014, but they will feature a very simple-to-use healing system we call "*The At Oneness Healing System*." In this book, you have witnessed the beginning of this new teaching series. The purpose of the webinars is to teach you a series of brand new advanced healing techniques that will be introduced in phases throughout the year.

Visit our website at: *http://www.worldserviceinstitute.org* and click "webinars" where indicated on the main page for our upcoming webinar schedule.

## Availability

Bob Fritchie is available for fee-based speaking engagements, plus development projects in the United States. Contact us by email: *infowsi@charter.net* to discuss your program needs.

We will also expand our international outreach program in the U.K., Europe, Australia and New Zealand when there is sufficient demand.

**Man is lost and is wandering in a jungle where real values have no meaning. Real values can have meaning to man only when he steps on to the spiritual path, a path where negative emotions have no use.**

~ Sai baba

# APPENDIX

# The 2013 Healing Yourself from Within Webinar Petitions

I've come to believe that each of us has a personal calling that's as unique as a fingerprint -- and that the best way to succeed is to discover what you love and then find a way to offer it to others in the form of service, working hard, and also allowing the energy of the universe to lead you.

~ Oprah Winfrey

# Appendix

Definitions for the words used in our Petitions can be sourced on our website, the *Free Healing Program* and our other healing books.

# 4 - Cycle Breathing Technique

When you do a Petition, you want to increase oxygenation of your system. If you can do deep breathing, then you may want to do this optional breathing exercise after you do every Petition. Repeat steps 1 - 4 below five times, or whenever you choose.

1. **Breathe in slowly and deeply.**
2. **Hold breath for 5 seconds.**
3. **Breathe out very slowly and empty your lungs completely.**
4. **Do not breathe in for 5 seconds.**

# The 2013 Petitions

These Petitions are best done when you can sit down on a chair with your feet flat on the floor and with your shoes off. If you are in a public place you may do the Petitions with your shoes on.

Remove all jewelry.

# BEING AT ONE WITH THE DIVINE

Sit in a quiet place.

Keep hands apart on chair arms or on a desktop.  Do not cross arms, clasp hands, or cross legs.

Eliminate distractions.  Turn off all equipment, e.g., TV, phones, and computers, and remove children and pets from the room.

Never do Petitions while driving.

Most people feel energy sensations in their bodies as they go through these healing Petitions.  That is normal.

Be patient with yourself.

Following are the 2013 Healing Yourself From Within Webinar Petitions and how to use them:

## 1. CHAKRA BALANCING

Use to balance your body energetically before and after the use of any other petition, or at any time to recharge yourself.

Take a deep breath.  Clasp hands together with your feet flat on the floor.

# Appendix

Say this **Chakra Balancing Petition** *aloud*:

> *"With my Spirit and the Divine Love that is within me, I ask that the Creator balance my system and my chakras according to the Creator's will."*

Then close your mouth, draw in breath and pulse your breath lightly through your nose as if trying to clear your nose. Wait about 10 seconds, then unclasp your hands. **This is the only Petition done with clasped hands.**

## 2. REMOVE LIMITED BELIEFS ABOUT DIVINE LOVE

Say this Petition *aloud* just *once* to release your limited beliefs!

> *"I acknowledge that I may not have correct definitions for DIVINE LOVE that the Creator wants for me.*
> *I ask that the Creator give me the experience and understanding that the Creator wants me to have, now and in the future, according to Divine will."*

# BEING AT ONE WITH THE DIVINE

Then close your mouth, draw in breath and pulse your breath lightly through your nose as if trying to clear your nose.

Begin 4-Cycle Breathing.

Wait at least 15 minutes, then do a Chakra Balancing Petition before doing any other Petition.

## 3. REMOVE LIMITED BELIEFS ABOUT THE CREATOR

Say this Petition *aloud* to release false beliefs and conscious and subconscious limited beliefs about the Creator.

> *"I acknowledge that I may not have correct definitions for the CREATOR that the Creator wants for me.*
> *I ask that the Creator give me the experience and understanding that the Creator wants me to have, now and in the future, according to Divine will."*

Then close your mouth, draw in breath and pulse your breath lightly through your nose as if trying to clear your nose.

# Appendix

Begin 4-Cycle Breathing.

Wait at least 15 minutes then do a Chakra Balancing Petition before doing any other Petition.

## 4. STAYING CONNECTED TO DIVINE LOVE

Your body works like a switch to turn the processing of Divine Love ON and OFF. You want your switch **ON** at all times. When you are angry or distracted, your switch turns **OFF** and you disconnect from Divine Love; healing stops.

People connect to Divine Love with Petitions, but some people disconnect as soon as they enter a public place because they get upset by something or someone.

This Petition will connect you *permanently* to Divine Love so that you do not shut down when exposed to an unloving act done to you by others or to yourself.

# BEING AT ONE WITH THE DIVINE

Say this **Staying Connected to Divine Love Petition** *aloud*.

> *"With my Spirit I send the Divine Love that is within me to my entire system.  I surrender my system to the control of my spirit.  I release to the Creator, ALL the causes that disconnect me from Divine Love and ask that the Creator lock my entire system in the ON position to continuously receive Divine Love according to the Creator's will."*

Then close your mouth, draw in breath and pulse your breath lightly through your nose as if trying to clear your nose.

Begin 4-Cycle Breathing.

Wait at least 15 minutes then do a Chakra Balancing Petition before doing any other Petition.

## 5. MENTAL CONSTRUCTS

Mental constructs are closely held beliefs that are not spiritually true.  All of the mental constructs you may have, plus those described by Petitions 2, 3 and 4 are incorporated in  this

# Appendix

**Mental Construct Petition.** Say *aloud*:

*"With my Spirit, I send the Divine Love that is within myself to my entire system. I surrender control of my system to my Spirit. I ask my spirit to go back to ALL the causes of ALL the mental constructs that are spiritually untrue and release ALL the causes of, and ALL the mental constructs themselves, to the Creator. I ask that the Creator fill me with Divine Love and heal my system according to the Creator's will."*

Then close your mouth, draw in breath and pulse your breath lightly through your nose as if trying to clear your nose.

Begin 4-Cycle Breathing.

Wait at least 15 minutes then do a Chakra Balancing Petition before doing any other Petition.

## 6. DIMENSIONAL VIBRATION

This Petition removes energy impacts that operate at a very high frequency. You need to

# BEING AT ONE WITH THE DIVINE

use this **Dimensional Vibration Petition** *only one time in your life*, early in the day after you do a Chakra Balancing. Say *aloud:*

*"With my Spirit I send the Divine Love that is within myself to my entire system. I surrender my system to the control of my spirit.*

*I release to the Creator - all the causes of any dimensional vibration misalignment from my existing life, or past lives, in my Soul, Mind, Body and Subtle Energy Bodies together with the symptoms caused by those misalignments. I ask that the Creator align my system to my Spirit, fill me with Divine Love and heal my system according to the Creator's will."*

Then close your mouth, draw in breath and pulse your breath lightly through your nose as if trying to clear your nose.

Begin 4-Cycle Breathing.

Wait at least 15 minutes then do a Chakra Balancing Petition before doing any other Petition.

# Appendix

## 7. UNLOVINGNESS

This is the primary petition that you will use (except for poisoning cases.) "Unlovingness" includes all thoughts, words, deeds and imprinted memories that may have impacted your system.

Say the **Unlovingness Petition** *aloud*:

**"With my Spirit, I send the Divine Love that is within myself to any unlovingness associated with my** (*name one symptom*) **and surrender my system to the control of my Spirit. I release all the causes of this unlovingness and the** (*name same symptom*) **itself to the Creator. I ask that the Creator fill me with Divine Love and heal my system according to the Creator's will."**

Then close your mouth, draw in breath and pulse your breath lightly through your nose as if trying to clear your nose.

Begin 4-Cycle Breathing.

Wait at least 15 minutes then do a Chakra Balancing Petition.

# BEING AT ONE WITH THE DIVINE

The *Unlovingness Petition* may take days to complete, so do not do another Petition of any kind (except for Chakra Balancing) for at least two days after your symptom has completely gone.

You can repeat the *Unlovingness Petition* if you want to, but that is unnecessary.

*Just do not change symptoms until the current symptom has totally corrected.*

*Do the Chakra Balancing Petition once or twice a day, usually morning and night.*

In the case of diseases, you will want to wait longer than 5 days to let your body heal. The healing itself is nearly instantaneous, but cell rejuvenation takes time. Most severe diseases should clear in 5 to 10 days after which you should confirm healing via medical test.

If an *emotional* condition persists on Day 6, ASK the Creator what you need to do.

If you are healing a *disease*, ASK the Creator *every day* what you should do.

Use this petition as often as you like each day.

# Appendix

## 8. FORGIVENESS

If you feel that you are having a problem forgiving yourself or the persons who have hurt you, use this petition. The symptoms that you may have had before doing the Petition such as pain or emotions usually dissolve immediately. Say *aloud:*

> *"With my Spirit, I send the Divine Love that is within myself to any memory or energy associated with my need to forgive myself and others and surrender my system to the control of my Spirit. I release ALL the causes of this unlovingness and the unforgiveness itself to the Creator. I ask that the Creator fill me with Divine Love and heal my system according to the Creator's will."*

Then close your mouth, draw in breath and pulse your breath lightly through your nose as if trying to clear your nose.

Begin 4-Cycle Breathing.

Wait 30 minutes then do a Chakra Balancing Petition followed by an Unlovingness Petition for your symptom.

# BEING AT ONE WITH THE DIVINE

## 9. STANDARD PETITION

This **Standard Petition** is used only if you are trying to correct a chemical poisoning in yourself from food, drink, bad air or chemicals that have penetrated your body. Say *aloud*:

*"With my Spirit, I send the Divine Love that is within myself to my (name one symptom) and surrender my system to the control of my Spirit. I release all the causes of my (name the same one symptom) and the (symptom) itself to the Creator. I ask that the Creator fill me with Divine Love and heal my system according to the Creator's will."*

Then close your mouth, draw in breath and pulse your breath lightly through your nose as if trying to clear your nose.

Begin 4-Cycle Breathing.

Wait 30 minutes then do a Chakra Balancing Petition.

The Standard Petition may take several days to complete, so do not do another Petition of any

220

## Appendix

kind for at least two days after your symptom has completely gone.

If the condition persists on Day 6, ASK the Creator what you need to do.

**Note: The Divine Love Petitions shown in this Appendix represent a complete healing system that you can use as indicated.**

*When love is given,
love should be returned;
anger is the thing
that gives no life.*

~ Hawaiian proverb

Lightning Source UK Ltd.
Milton Keynes UK
UKOW04f0947270515

252365UK00001B/133/P